ASK Ernest

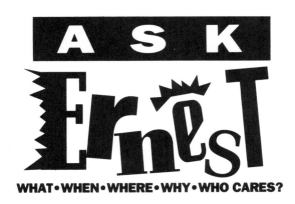

Ernest P. Worrell

Rutledge Hill Press
Nashville, Tennessee

Published in Nashville, Tennessee, by Rutledge Hill Press, Inc., 211 Seventh Avenue North, Nashville, Tennessee 37219

Library of Congress Cataloging-in-Publication Data

Ask Ernest: What, when, where, why, who cares/Ernest P. Worrell.
    p.   cm.
   ISBN 1-55853-247-1
   1. American wit and humor. 2. Worrell, Ernest P. (Fictitious character) I. Title: What, when, where, why, who cares.
PN6162.A78   1993   93-30370
818′.5402 — dc20   CIP

Printed in the United States of America

1 2 3 4 5 6 7 8 — 98 97 96 95 94 93

TABLE OF CONTENTS

LEGAL PUBLIC NOTICE

Susan Brown
Andrew Morris
Jade Nowak
Glenn Petsch
Templeton
Mary Thompson
Mariellen Sasseen
Steve Brown
Leiate Smiley
Kristy McIntosh
David A. Butler

Hi Neighbor!

INTRODUCTION

Ernest P. Worrell is a full-time registered nurse with extensive experience in the care of persons with eating disorders. In addition to his vast entertainment, movie and television career, Ernest is also the proprietor of Miss Edna's Moon Pie in the Sky in Scotchguard, Ohio. This restaurant and bakery specializes in single serving, frozen dinner entrees and processed fish bait. His previous books are *The American Bed & Breakfast Cookbook for Raising Your Sodium Level*, *The Book of Knawledge* and *Family Diesel Repair Made Simple with Dr. Otto.*

ASK Ernest

WHAT DO YOU SAY TO SOMEONE WITH A BAD HAIRCUT?

"Have you been sick?"

"Who cut your hair? John Deere?"

"Did you get the license number?"

"Are you gonna sue?"

"Now I remember why I don't like Poodles!"

"So you're the one who took my electric hedge clippers!"

"How many people live up there?"

"Nice hat."

SCHOOL BUS SURVIVAL

- Don't bring your dog.
- Never let a short person on before you.
- Always get a window seat in the back if the driver seems unusually sedated.
- Never eat your lunch on the way to school.
- If sick, throw up on someone wearing vinyl.
- Never put super glue on the gas pedal.
- Always carve someone else's name on the seat.
- Never, ever sit next to a guy wearing a turban and carrying a live grenade.
- No pressed ham.

"IN" THINGS

TO STAY OUT OF

INfernos

INsecticides

INfirmaries

INquests   INsurance Scandals   INternational INtrigue

INfections   INdiscreet INterludes   INtestinal INflammations

INternal Combustion Engines   INcinerators   INdigestion

INferiority Complexes   INdustrial Accidents

INquisitions

INcome Tax Evasion

INfantry Maneuvers

INeptitude   INcarceration

INsane Asylums

INdia Ink   INgrown Toenails

IN-law's Arguments

FOLK MEASUREMENTS

HERE'S ONE FOR GOOD MEASURE

You know, Vernon, folk measurements are a lot more accurate than most people might think. And especially when you're short of precise measuring instruments, they come in very handy. Mostly, it's just a good eye, a little instinct and lots of common sense. Here's a good guide to measurements that might prove useful when you're caught without your yardstick on you.

⊗ A blink of an eye is markedly faster than you can say Jack Robinson. Yet, it is only a shade quicker than you can say spit.

⊗ Greased lightning equals the speed of light plus about 15% to account for the grease. That's almost twice as fast as a bat out of hell. Though it was always considered that a bat out of hell was comparable to excrement running through a goose.

⊗ "Like he was shot out of a cannon" usually refers to speed, i.e. velocity; but this can as well refer to a scrunched facial expression or a reaction to a kiss from a rabid dog.

⊗ You can pinch a bit of a tad from a smidgen. Yet, you can't pinch a smidgen from a tad of a bit. And it is virtually impossible to bite a tad of a smidgen of a bit. Plus, a smidgen of an inkling is usually indecipherable. So, in order of size, it's pinch, tad, bit, smidgen and inkling.

⊗ "The whole nine yards" is the same amount as "a full load." It is less, though, than the whole kit and kaboodle and a little more than you can shake a stick at. Therefore, you can shake a stick at the whole kit and kaboodle and it will still be considerably less than the whole nine yards.

⊗ Someone who doesn't have both oars in the water is a little smarter than someone whose pilot light is out. Surprisingly though, someone whose elevator doesn't go to the top floor will probably lose to someone whose pilot light is out in a spelling bee.

⊗ A screen door is less intelligent than a fence post, and a fence post is much dumber than a bucket of rocks. But, still, you can't be dumber than a bucket of rocks and have both oars in the water. 🐓

THE DO'S AND DON'TS OF EATING SUSHI

DON'T ask for ketchup.

DO remember: Saki's for sippin' and soy's for dippin'.

DON'T ask what the little pink thing in the center is.

DO bring a small fork as a back-up utensil.

DON'T peel off the black wrapper holdin' it together.

DO try to use just one hand with chopsticks.

DON'T think about what you're chewin' on, just swallow!

DO know CPR because somebody's bound to faint when the bill comes.

Career Corner: Skywriting

We're talkin' high tech communications! Super-sonic skywriting... it's a space age necessity... 'cause when folks start vacationing on the moon... they're gonna be looking for exit signs, clean restrooms and campground directions... but you can't put a billboard in space, so you gotta write directly on the sky! Yeah, skywriting is a great career if you got upward mobility... KNOWHUTIMEAN?

"can skywriters take a correspondence course?"

THINGS YOU SHOULD
ASK YOURSELF...

...When you walk
into a dentist's office:

Is anyone screaming?

Is there blood on the floor?

Does the dentist look happy
or depressed?

Does the chair face the door?

Is there plenty of laughing gas?

Could the visit be put off
a few more days?

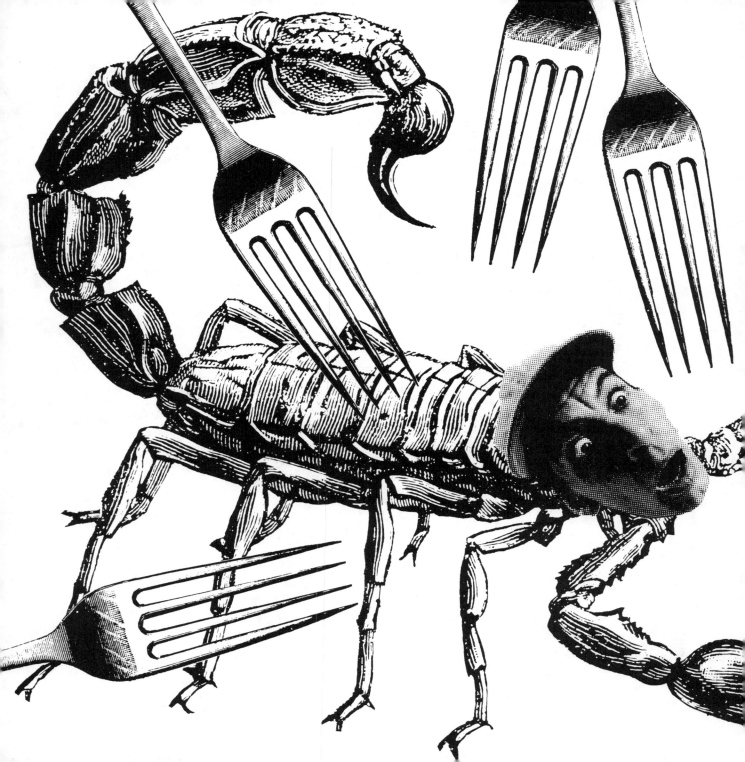

HOW TO EAT A
SCORPION

Vern, the scorpion has been consumed by mankind for thousands of years and goes by many names. Personally, I prefer the name Dessert Lobster, as most gourmet cooks do. But you might call 'em Sand Shrimp, Rock Roach, Navajo Caviar, or Buffalo Crab. Before you dig into these things, Vernon, you've got to get your mind straight. Think of this sorta like your first date -- after it was all over, girls didn't seem so bad... KnoWhutImean?

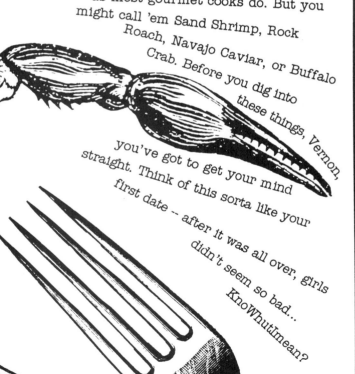

Just follow these nine steps...and remember to order up a pot full, 'cause these things are like warts, Vern, they'll grow on you.

1. Twist off the pinchers.

2. Crack 'em with a mallet.

3. Bend off the tail.

4. Remove the stinger from tail.

5. Put a chopstick into the tail.

6. Push chopstick 'til meat comes out.

7. Destroy the body.

8. Use legs for a straw.

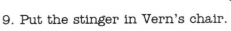

9. Put the stinger in Vern's chair.

TABLE MANNERS

SOMETIMES WHEN YOU'RE EATING MEAT, YOU END UP WITH UGLY, CHEWY THINGS IN YOUR MOUTH THAT YOU DIDN'T INTEND TO BE EATING. IF YOU FIGURE IT'S LESS THAN AN INCH OR TWO LONG, JUST PULL IT OUT WITH YOUR FINGERS AND PUT IT ON THE SIDE OF YOUR PLATE. DON'T EXAMINE IT TOO LONG IN FRONT OF YOUR HOST. IF IT'S LONGER THAN TWO INCHES AND YOU DON'T LIKE THE FEEL OF IT, JUST STAND UP AND SAY, "I THINK I'M GONNA BE SICK," AND LEAVE THE ROOM.

WEIRD HAIR IN THE TWENTIETH CENTURY!

DON KING
MOE
HITLER
KOJAK
DAVID LETTERMAN
EINSTEIN
VERNON
CURLY
RIP TORN
CYNDI LAUPER
COUSIN IT
WILLARD SCOTT
LIBERACE
ALFAFA
MR. T
PHYLLIS DILLER
LASSIE
STEVIE WONDER
LARRY
KOOL & THE GANG
TINA TURNER
MR. PRESIDENT

These little Velcros, found only where weather is available, are a strange breed. The mother Velcro has little hook-like hairs all over her back and stomach with the little hooks always pointing to magnetic north. In contrary, the hairs of the Velcro young always point south thus allowing them to hook up to the mother from time to time for meals and protection. The father Velcro's hair has no claws to pry the mother and her young apart after feeding, etc. Once a year the Velcro species shed their skin for the benefit of mankind and the shoe industry.

HOW DOES VELCRO WORK?

Door Number 3 Or What's Behind The Curtain?

If you find yourself at a crowded party with a mouthful of black licorice and a guest asks you to comment on world over-population and starvation, don't spit the juice in the house plants. If you have to, just sneeze real good into a dark-colored curtain.

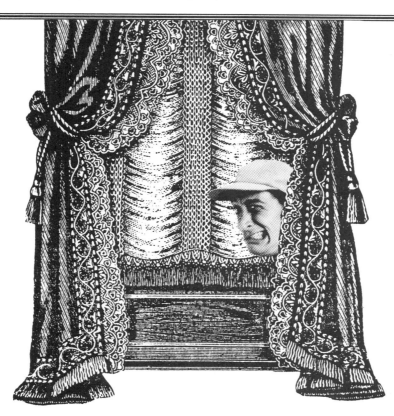

Bone Up On The Facts

The funny **BONE** is not really a **BONE** at all, but rather a small nerve.

That member of the human body with the most **BONES** is the foot. (If we're talking "feet," you could just about double that number.)

That member with the fewest **BONES** is the human nose.

Speaking of the human knows, the brain has no **BONES**. It is, however the source of most all **BONERS**.

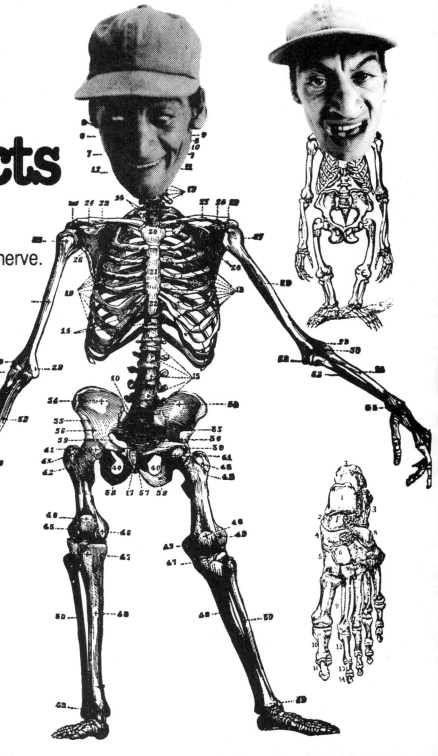

the ANIMAL KINGDOM

- The platypus has a duck bill, otter fur, webbed feet, lays eggs, secretes a milky substance, eats its own weight in worms every day, smells like a wet dog and can count all his friends on one hand.

- Woodpecker finches of the Galapagos Islands use cactus thorns and twigs as tools to probe in tree trunks and branches for insects, but you can leave a complete set of fine surgical instruments out over night and they won't even touch 'em.

- A ruby-throated hummingbird has 940 feathers. It takes 906,470 ruby-throated hummingbirds to make one medium down jacket.

- Lizards are better at controlling insect and spider populations than insecticides, but their short shelf-life makes them impractical.

- Ostriches, the world's largest bird, can growl like a lion and hiss like a snake. A few have even been seen doing a pretty good John Wayne.

- Mink ranching was a popular, get-rich-quick scheme brought to the South by carpet-baggers after the Civil War. The craze spread rapidly through the West as the "minkboys" displayed their considerable skills in small but lively rodeos.

- The 20th Amendment, known as the "Lame Duck Amendment," was railroaded through Congress in 1933 by a militant wing of the Audubon Society, creating the now familiar barrier-free wetlands in our national park system.

WHAT TO WEAR

Relish in every hot lick on that flaming accordian ...it's Polka Night at the Moose Lodge and you're the envy of all the meeses. Especially when you arrive decked in this classic, basic white top, complete with embroidered trim and lace up front. Kielbasa stains on the front are optional, yet considered fashionably acceptable in most parts of Europe and Chicago.

Do you enjoy full cable hook-up? Getting caught with *Leave It To Beaver* reruns on at 3am? Then this non-absorbent asbestos/polyester blend comfort shirt should fit right into your schedule. Immaculately tailored for a man of the tube, it easily repels mustard and ketchup stains, literally flirts with the danger of a Salisbury Steak TV dinner, and welcomes the chance to fight off warm root beer droppings.

Backyard chores will be a snap when you're donned in this stylish, contemporary long-sleeve flannel shirt with our exclusively patented "Mr. Sweat-Away" arm pit protector. Steel-toed shoes, before 8:00pm, always add that special distinctive finishing touch.

WHERE.

So, you want to be a sheep herder? Well, you'll have those woolly waifs "flocking" to you for miles when you gather them in this 9-button, blue, puff-sleeve shepherd shirt. Commands respect from even the hardest to herd. (Accessory suggestion: a large, blue sheep dog.)

Be the envy of your team when you arrive in this perfect, light-weight, 80% cotton/40% rayon/12% polyester bowling shirt. That 7-10 split should be no problem, as the arm pits expand and contract with the amount of English spin you put on each and every roll. Plus, each shirt comes with your name stitched in thick red over the front pocket. (Send name printed in English with each order. Spelling counts towards "Super Bowl" discount).

You gotta trust me on this one, Vern. If ever you're in doubt as to what to wear for any occasion, choose the look that fits any-time, anyplace. Basic blue jeans, basic jean vest, basic khaki hat, basic grey T-shirt. Basically, this ensemble covers all the bases. KnoWhutImean?

*Remember, Vern. Try and remove all straight pins before wearing.

THE KITCHEN MAGICIAN

One day li'l Ernie was helpin' Mom Worrell bake some white bread. She kneeded (Ha! Ha!) to let the dough rise for **15** minutes. But all she had was a **7** minute and an **11** minute hour glass. If the dough rose more than **15** minutes, the bread would be ruint and li'l Ernie would have to go to bed hungry. How did li'l Ernie start and stop the timers for exactly **15** minutes and save the white bread? (Answer On Some Other Page... Maybe.)

THE PROPER CARE AND TRAINING OF YOUR PETS

Cats can keep themselves clean. You can put out a little guest towel and a bar of soap, but don't bother, they won't use them.

To get rid of the hair on the furniture, don't shave your cat. They get so mad it's just not worth it.

It's possible to train your cat to use the toilet, but it's a whole lot easier to get your family to use the litter box.

The vacuum cleaner works great to clean the bird cage. Just make sure the little feller's got his perch belt on.

If you find your goldfish floating belly-up in the bowl, don't panic. It may just be an attention-getting device. Give it a couple days, and if there's no change, put a splint on it.

Some people dress their dogs up in little clothes to make them feel special, but dogs hate this. It makes them feel silly. A little lipstick and eyeliner goes a long way.

If your dog is always begging at the table, get him some sunglasses and a tin cup. He'll either be too humiliated to beg, or he'll start earning his own keep.

PROPER FLEA MARKET ETIQUETTE

You break it, you bought it.

Buy low, sell high.

Never buy cosmetics from an overweight woman with facial hair.

If you've never seen it, buy it–
you'll probably never see it again.

Never pay the asking price.

Park only in designated areas.

Always exit the same door
you came in.

Bring your own toilet paper.

Contrary to popular belief,
there are no fleas–only
human parasites.

Controlling That Sweet Tooth

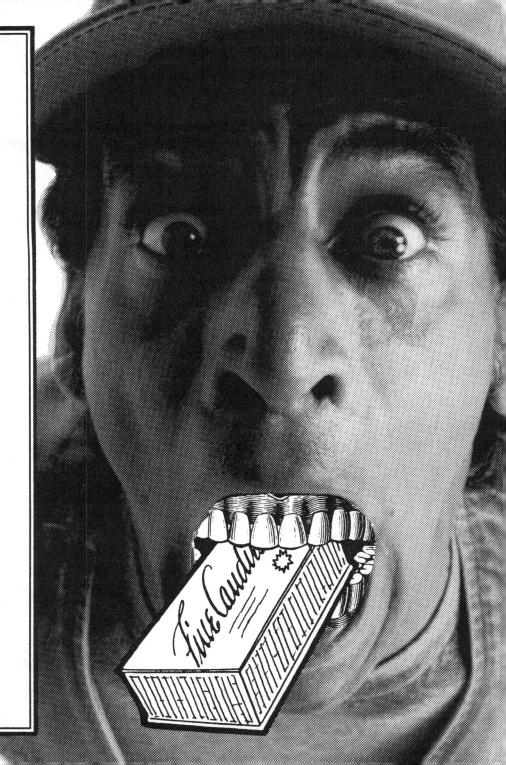

When someone offers you a piece of candy from a box of assorted chocolates, you should never take a bite off more than 4 pieces to find one with peanut butter.

NUTS

Ernest Picks This Week's Top 20

Best Songs to Fall Asleep By (or is that Asheep?)

1. Embraceable Ewe
2. Ewe Are the Sunshine of My Life
3. Ewe Made Me Love Ewe
5. To Know, Know, Know Ewe Is to Love, Love, Love Ewe
6. Ewe Ain't Nothin' But a Hound Dog
7. I Get a Kick Out of Ewe
9. Have Ewe Ever Been Lonely
10. Ewe Light Up My Life
11. Getting to Know Ewe
12. I've Got Ewe Under My Skin
14. Ewe Keep Me in Granola
15. Do Ewe Know the Way to San Jose
16. Ewe, Ewe, Ewe
17. Ewe Send Me
19. Nobody But Ewe
20. I.O. Ewe

COLD

HANDS

WARM

HEART

Yer body pumps blood on a
priority system. Yer highest
priority is yer head ('cause that's
where yer cranium maximus
is located). Then, once yer head is
warm, the next priority is yer
torso...comprendo? So now yer
head 'n body's warm, but yer
hands 'n feet are cold, and that's
where they get the sayin'
"Cold hands, Warm heart!"

NAME GAMES

Vern, you ever run into somebody at K-Mart or out at the tractor pull whose face is familiar but whose name just don't come up on your cerebral Rol-a-dex? KnoWhutImean?

Used to happen to me all the time, Vern.

That's why I have developed the following 86% foolproof methods to prevent such socially devastatin' situations from intruding into my carefully constructed lifestyle. (In other words, Vern, here are some things you can do when you can't remember somebody's name.)

HELLO
My Name Is:
Ernest

1. Avoid Speaking At All
   A feller can't notice you don't remember his name if you pretend that you don't remember him at *all*. So when you run into somebody whose face is in your memory banks but whose name won't come when you call it, just smile and walk right on past him. He'll either think you're deaf, blind, stupid, or a combination of all three. (Of course, the joke will be on him, Vern, because you *know* you're not deaf or blind.)
2. If it's a formal cultural event, see if you can sneak around behind him and get a look at the back of his belt.
3. Before he gets a chance to talk, whip out your petition to make Fencing With Power Tools a recognized event at the 1996 Olympics. When he signs it, you can get a look at his name.
4. Look for little initials on this person's shirt pocket or cufflinks or purse. Sometimes these initials are all you need to jog your memory, especially if the person whose name you forgot turns out to be J.C. Penney or B.F. Goodrich or E.F. Hutton.
5. Before he finds out you don't know his name, work the topic around to gambling and bet him that your social security card makes a better poker hand than his does. When he shows you his card, you can peek at the name while you're collecting your money. (And you *will* collect money, Vern. All it takes is an ink eraser, a steady hand and a red felt tip marker. Nuff said—KnoWhutImean?)
6. When all else fails, call everybody VERN!

Shooting Stars

Shooting Stars are really shot-down stars. It's their last blaze of glory. But what worries me is who's shooting the stars? Is the man in the moon a sharp-shooter? Does he even win a prize if he hits one? Can you stuff a star and hang it in the den? Is this where starfish come from? Should there be Gun Control in outer space?

TO BE CONTINUED...

Take A Look At The Movies You Can Rent In A Grocery Store.

THE GHOST AND MR. CHICKEN

LOOKING FOR MR. GOODBAR

THE APPLE DUMPLING GANG

 THE ONION FIELD

HAMLET

THE ATTACK OF THE KILLER TOMATOES

 GREASE AND GREASE II

CHILDREN OF THE CORN

THE MARX BROTHERS' ANIMAL CRACKERS

PORKY'S REVENGE

MEATBALLS

THE GRAPES OF WRATH

FOOD FOR THOUGHT

 BANANAS

A CLOCKWORK ORANGE

GOODBYE MR. CHIPS

LEARN IT OR BURN IT
-with Ernest

WALNUT CARP

1 10 lb. carp   1 2' x 6' walnut board   2 T. paprika   1 stick of butter
1 smidgen cayenne pepper   1 iotas ginger root   1 sprig parsley

Broil at 350° for 20 minutes or until carp yells "Uncle!" Remove from oven, salt and pepper to your liking. Then, throw the fish away. Serve with diet cola. Feeds 50 woodpeckers.

Everybody's gotta have wheels. My personal choice is a lean, mean pick-em-up machine... KnoWhuttImean? (Have you ever tried feedin' cows from the back of your car?) It's real nice to have a truck you can be proud of, so your ol' buddy Ernest is gonna give you some helpful hints on havin' the meanest machine around.

TRUCK BED:
- Chairs for the kids to sit on.
- Several empty oil cans.
- Jumper cable.
- A coon hound.

INSIDE:
- Gun rack with umbrella.
- Four on the floor.
- Decorative screen on back window, like a rodeo scene, migratin' geese, or an armadillo.

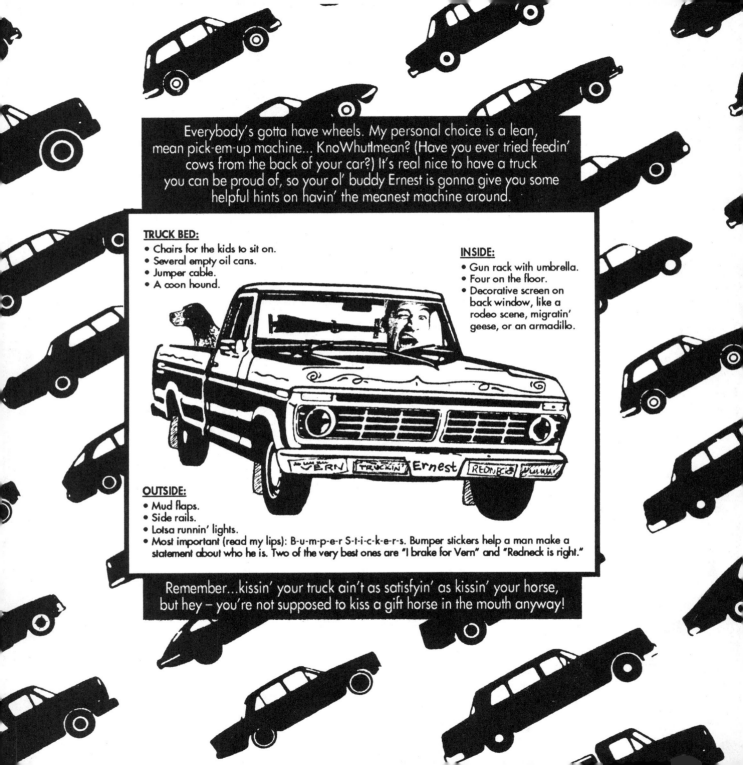

OUTSIDE:
- Mud flaps.
- Side rails.
- Lotsa runnin' lights.
- Most important (read my lips): B-u-m-p-e-r S-t-i-c-k-e-r-s. Bumper stickers help a man make a statement about who he is. Two of the very best ones are "I brake for Vern" and "Redneck is right."

Remember...kissin' your truck ain't as satisfyin' as kissin' your horse, but hey – you're not supposed to kiss a gift horse in the mouth anyway!

WHY DO THEY CALL IT --

Why do they call them mobile homes when nobody ever moves them?

Why do they call them ice cubes when lots of times they're round?

Why do they call it taking a shower when you always stay in the same place? You haven't gone anywhere and it's still there when you're through.

Why, when you use a mop, do they call it mopping, but when you use a broom, you don't get to call it brooming?

Why do they bother with calling them hot air balloons? I've never known anyone to get them confused with cold air balloons.

Why do they call famous people stars, but never suns or moons or comets?

Why do they call it playing the piano when you have to take lessons to learn how to do it?

Why do they call them caution lights when that's when everybody goes even faster?

Why do they call it personal wealth when nobody I know has any?

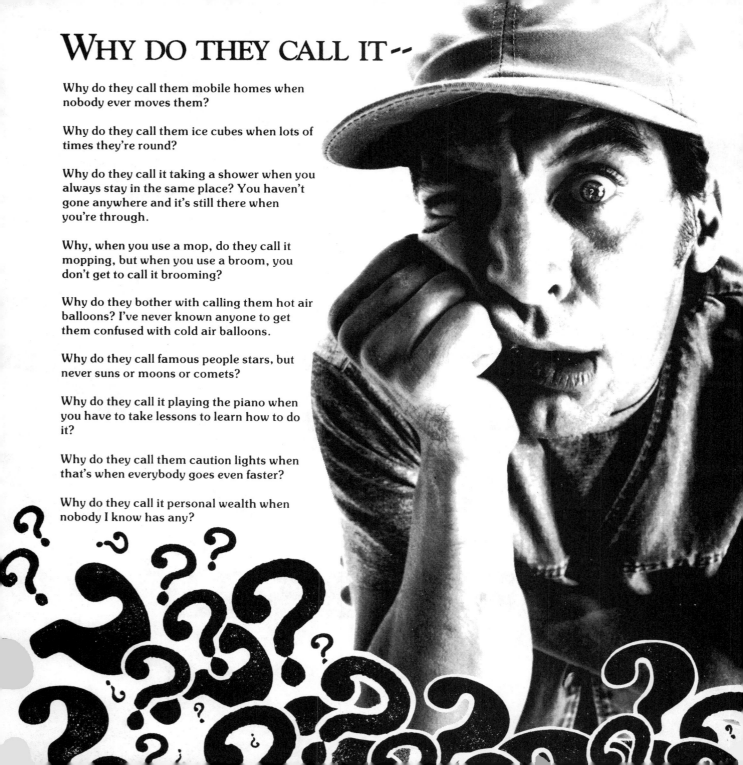

The Things We Can Do Without:

Smiley faces
Slide shows
Carp
Lucky rabbit feet
Club Med
Brussels sprouts
Soap on a rope
Leap year
I ♥ bumper stickers
Income tax
Three's Company re-runs

The Things We Need More Of:

Wrestling on TV
Power tools
Mr. Microphone
Record offers
Junk mail
Chili
Newsletters
Corn dogs
Rest stops
Velcro shoes
Credit
Andy Griffith re-runs

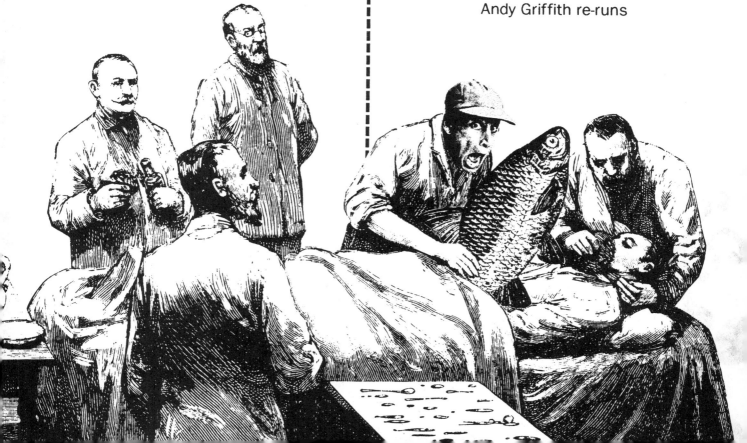

Everybody talks about stress in the fast-paced city life, but country folks have to deal with stress, too. It's not just one big picnic, y'know. I've rated some common country stress events from 1 to 100. If you score more than 300 points per year, you might as well dig yourself a deep hole.

Lawn is getting kinda' long	5
Date on milk carton expired	5
Bottom falls out of trash bag	6
Neighbor's dogs won't shut up	11
Carpet starting to look worn in front of sofa	8
Porch swing develops a bad squeak	11
Slept through "Wheel of Fortune"	17
Didn't win Publisher's Clearing House Sweepstakes	12
A card is missing from the good deck	17
First Christmas with fake tree	18
Daughter elopes	12
Your new shoes weren't in the mail again today	25
Goats eat the vinyl top off your car	30
Family reunion overrun by neighbor's dogs	37
Shear a pin on your fishing motor—lose propeller	40
The cows break out during Super Bowl	54
Daughter elopes during Super Bowl	12
Cat has litter on your suede jacket	55
Power goes out—you eat 20 TV dinners in 3 days	50
Brother-in-law backs your pickup into your septic tank	75
Brother-in-law gets nose broken	2
Wife spends night at her mother's	70
No TV dinners left	78
Wind blows TV antenna down	87

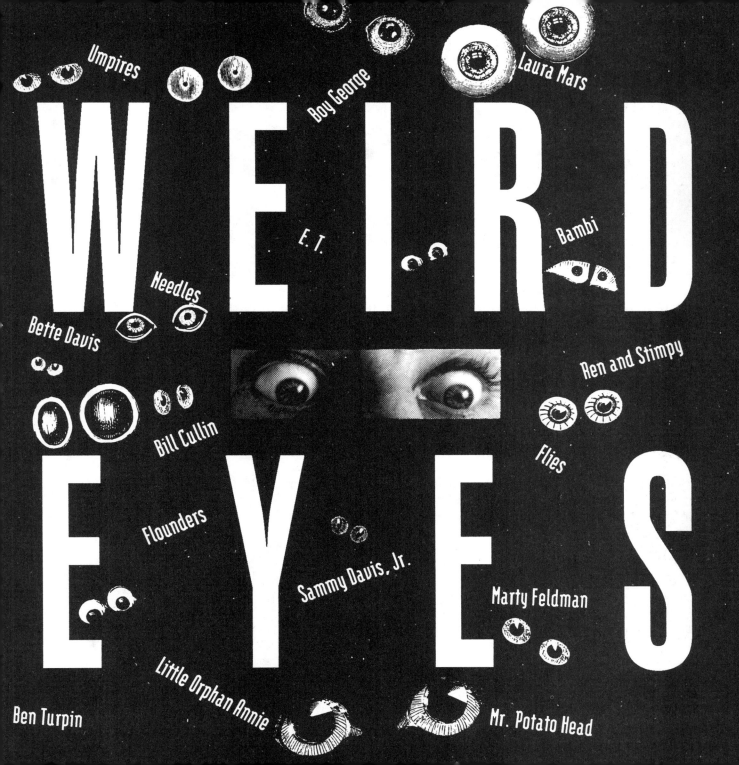

WEIRD EYES

Umpires
Boy George
Laura Mars
E.T.
Bambi
Needles
Bette Davis
Ren and Stimpy
Bill Cullin
Flies
Flounders
Sammy Davis, Jr.
Marty Feldman
Ben Turpin
Little Orphan Annie
Mr. Potato Head

The Origin of Italian Food Names

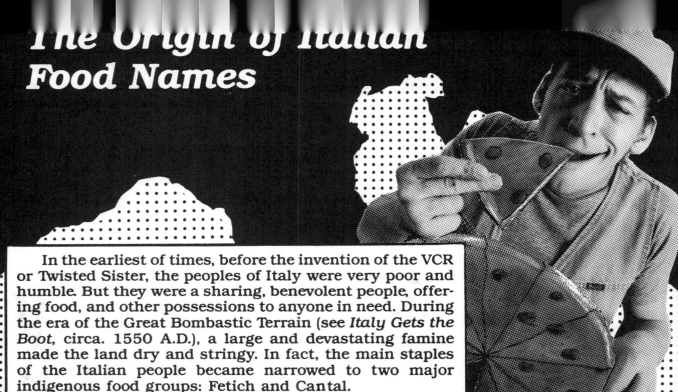

In the earliest of times, before the invention of the VCR or Twisted Sister, the peoples of Italy were very poor and humble. But they were a sharing, benevolent people, offering food, and other possessions to anyone in need. During the era of the Great Bombastic Terrain (see *Italy Gets the Boot,* circa. 1550 A.D.), a large and devastating famine made the land dry and stringy. In fact, the main staples of the Italian people became narrowed to two major indigenous food groups: Fetich and Cantal.

It became a common call through the small dry villages as nomadic families would stick their heads through the thatched doors of homes and ask of the owner… "Fetich? Any?" or "Cantal? Loan me?"

Soon a great Providence came over the entire land with the invention of THE PIZZA PIE! Now there was more Fetich and Catal than twelve countries of the same size could possibly ever eat. Plates were piled high at every meal. Women grew fat and happy, men fat and lazy, children…well, just fat. Yet, the peoples of Italy never forgot their ancestors and the great famine.

So today, these calls are used as names for these Italian dishes, though modernization has caused each to be run together. So next time you're in an Italian restaurant ordering one of these favorites, as you stuff your face, leave half to be thrown away, and crawl home to sleep on satin sheets, remember the echoing distant cries of a once near-dead people, vainly pleading to merely save the frail lives of their families and children.

And get you a pizza pie to go. KnoWhutImean?

Never leave your dog in the car on a hot day unless you plan to eat him.

Where in the world would we be without
HORMONES?

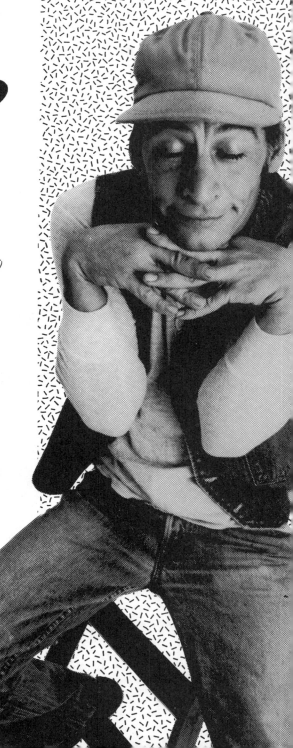

Without our hormones, we'd probably all be hairless, squeaky-voiced runts with perfectly clear [face] and no desire whatsoever to take [cheerleader] to the prom. But thank goodness Sir Isaac Oxyten took the time to discover hormones.

In the year [1753], somewhere just north of [Idaho] Ol' Isaac was sitting right under an adolescent perched in a chocolate covered donut [tree] when a hormone the size of a [watermelon] fell on him. In that [lightning bolt], growing up and zits with minds of their own were discovered. Sir Isaac went on to later discover I.D. bracelets and the [fryer].

T R A V E L

To liven up a long bus ride, wear a crash helmet and tell everyone the driver is your older brother.

When checking out of a motel, always take as many towels as you can. The motel expects it and they also enjoy charging your credit card $200 per towel. And if you don't, the towels just eventually back up so bad that the whole place could blow at any minute.

If you see a hitch-hiker, lock all your doors, pull up next to him and look him over for a good 5 minutes before driving off in a cloud of dust.

Just because there's a lot of trucks parked outside a cafe doesn't mean the food is good, any more than a bunch of chefs parked outside a garage means there's a good mechanic inside.

BACKYARD BAR-B-Q
With Ernest!
Learn it or Burn it

SPAM-KA-BOB
1 large can of SPAM
5 Jalapeno peppers
2 medium 'maters
Canned pineapple chunks
Coat hangers

Cut SPAM in 2" cubes. Cut up all the rest of the junk. Saw and use only the bottoms of coat hangers. Mix up and insert coat hangers thru all the pieces. Grill over Mesquite coals for 45 min. Turning and burning, or until coat hangers brand your finger tips. Serves 4 to 5 desperate people. Note: for your formal occasions, call it SPAM-KA-ROBERT.

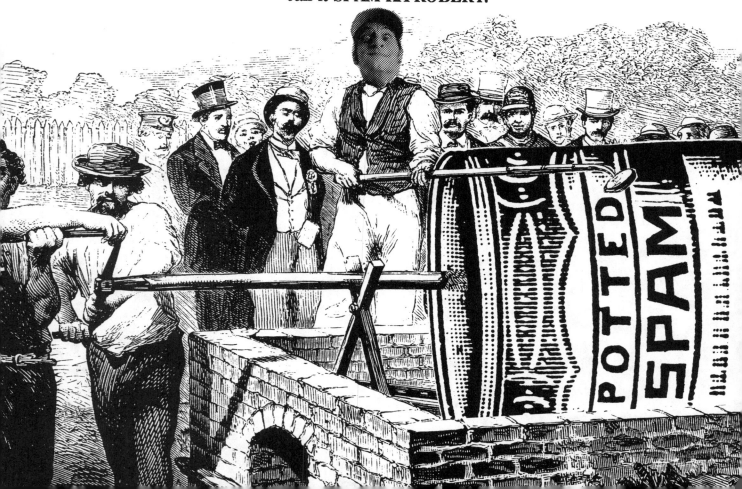

How to make a KITE

STEP 1 Get some yardsticks and an old sheet, baling wire and lots of string and scotch tape, and make it look like this...

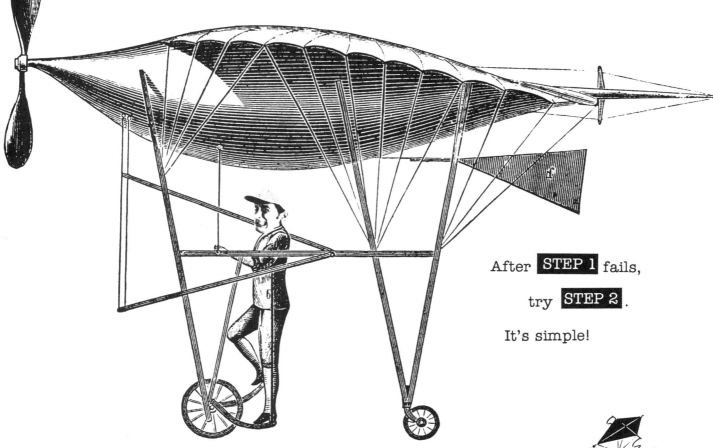

After **STEP 1** fails,

try **STEP 2**.

It's simple!

STEP 2 Borrow five bucks from Vern or get an advance on your allowance....whatever's easier. And go buy one at the five and dime. Why do they call 'em five and dimes? Exactly! 'Cause you can't buy anything for a dime! (And remember, Vern...don't tie small pets to kite tails and don't look at your armpits in public.)

Hey Vern! Let's check and see what kind of personality you got. Or better yet let's see IF you got one at all! So answer these simple questions. But answer 'em honest, Vern. After all, it's for your own good.

1. If you were floating down a lazy river on a raft with the soft summer breeze of a July afternoon whispering through your hair, what fruit would you want to be?
☐ A) A fig
☐ B) A date
☑ C) A pomegranate

2. If you saw an old friend from grade school collapse at a train station from heat exhaustion and begin foaming at the mouth, you would...
☐ A) Buy a ticket on the NEXT train immediately.
☐ B) Run grab a grinder's organ, tie a small rope around his neck and begin collecting spare change from the people standing around watching.
☑ C) Remind him that he still had your social studies notebook and that you needed it back.

3. If you had one cow and the farmer next to you had three cows, what color would you paint your barn?
☐ A) Blue
☑ B) A shade of mauve
☐ C) Go with the Zen philosophy and realize that all color is merely an illusion

4. If you could be any tree, what would you be?
☑ A) An oak tree
☑ B) A weeping willow tree
☐ C) A shoe tree

5. When you're in a crowded room of people you don't know, all dressed in bunny suits, you usually...
☐ A) Try and act inconspicuous, mingling through the crowd discussing the latest *Consumer Reports* issue.
☑ B) Ask for purple lettuce and stand in a corner.
☐ C) Make sure you get all their names spelled correctly for the local newspaper.

6. When a large bearded man approaches you in a dark alleyway wearing a stocking mask and carrying a loaded pearl-handled gun, you assume...
☐ A) That he is collecting for UNICEF.
☑ B) That he merely wants your opinion on the state of affairs in a small Middle Eastern country.
☐ C) His second mortgage.

7. If you are out on a blind date, how much money do you figure you must spend on the lady before it is appropriate to expect a good-night kiss?
☐ A) $5-$10
☑ B) Over $50
☐ C) Spend $5-$10 and tell her it was $50. Remember, she's blind and won't know the difference.

8. If you were stranded on a desert island with only a VCR, a 14″ color TV and a power generator, what movie cassette would you want with you?
☐ A) Herbie Goes to Monte Carlo
☑ B) The Ernest Film Festival
☑ C) National Geographic presents "The Water Beetle: Friend or Foe?"

9. If you were to describe yourself as a famous movie actor, who would it be?
☑ A) Gary Coleman
☑ B) Rin Tin Tin
☐ C) The Elephant Man

10. How many of these personality tests have you taken in the past year?
☐ A) 365
☐ B) Is that what this is?
☑ C) Only this one, and believe me, it's my last.

ABOUT VACATIONS: Three days where you want to be is better than three weeks where you don't. Travel agents work for the Russian KGB. And never, ever drink from the waterbed.

ABOUT NEWSPAPERS: If you only read the headlines, you'll know more than somebody who doesn't. If you use only the headlines to paper train your puppy, it will take twice as long as if you had used the whole paper.

ABOUT SPELLING: Sumtymes it duzent madder— U kan styl git yur poynt akross.

THINGS MY MOTHER NEVER TOLD ME ABOUT

Three things I never see enough of, Vern. And that's midget rasslers, income tax refunds and bumper stickers. Now, two of these things I can't do nothin' about, but when it comes to bumper stickers, I think it's the duty of every red-blooded, four-wheeled human bean to cover every square inch of bumper in this country with socially relevant, intellectually stimulatin' information for the **90**'s.

All That Glitters Is Not Chrome

See Rock City

Hey Vern!
NEXT TIME TALK TO YOUR OL' BUDDY ERNEST FIRST.

THIS CAR POOL HAS BEEN DRAINED

My Teachers Wouldn't Pass Me...
Why Should You?

Only You Can Prevent
Forest Tuckers

I'M NOT WEARING ANY PANTS

HONK
IF YOU LOVE NOISE

REMEMBER THE, UH...THE...

What...Are You
Behind Me Again?

And remember, Vern...the sticky side goes down.

A BICENTENNIAL BRIEF

GEORGE WASHINGTON'S TEETH WERE BELIEVED TO BE MADE OF WOOD, BUT IN REALITY, GEORGE'S TEETH WERE MADE FROM SPANISH TILE. GEORGE HAD THIS THING FOR SOUTH-OF-THE-BORDER ARCHITECTURE, SO ON HIS VISITS TO TIJUANA, HE WOULD ALWAYS DRINK ROOT BEER MADE FROM JUMPING BEANS WHICH ROTTED EVERY TOOTH IN HIS HEAD AND OFTEN CAUSED LONG PERIODS OF MENTAL DEPRESSION. BECAUSE OF HIS OUTRAGEOUS APPETITE FOR BEEF JERKY, HE DECIDED TO ACQUIRE THE SERVICES OF MEXICO'S MOST CELEBRATED DENTIST, DR. JOSÉ LAFARQWAI WHO, TO THIS DAY, SWEARS UP AND DOWN THAT GEORGE WASHINGTON WAS INDEED A HABITUAL LIAR.

What To Give The Person Who Has Everything.

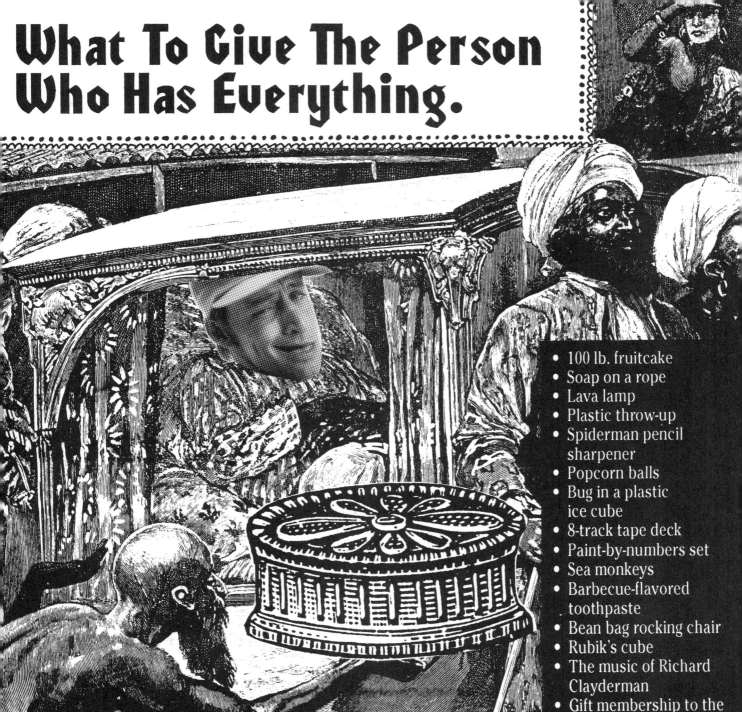

- 100 lb. fruitcake
- Soap on a rope
- Lava lamp
- Plastic throw-up
- Spiderman pencil sharpener
- Popcorn balls
- Bug in a plastic ice cube
- 8-track tape deck
- Paint-by-numbers set
- Sea monkeys
- Barbecue-flavored toothpaste
- Bean bag rocking chair
- Rubik's cube
- The music of Richard Clayderman
- Gift membership to the Ernest Fan Club
- A nasty cold

COOKING SAFETY TIP NO.9

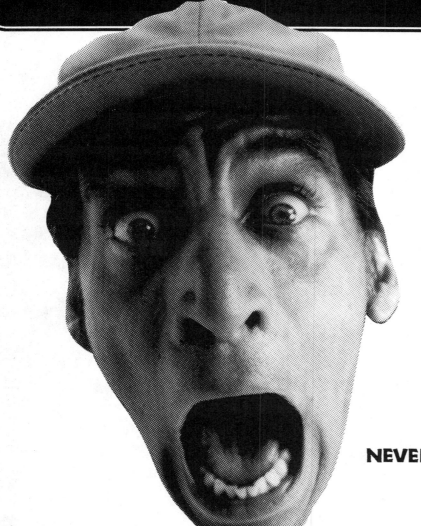

NEVER COOK BACON NAKED!

CARTUNES

not all cartoons are on tv SOME OF THE VERY BEST HAPPEN IN THE FAMILY WAGON

blue suede brake shoes I LEFT MY HEART IN A MONTE CARLO i'm snow tired of you CARDUST rock around the cylinder block THE NIGHT THE HEADLIGHTS WENT OUT IN GEORGIA you are the sunroof of my life I HEARD IT THROUGH THE GAS LINE don't go braking my heart I'VE GOT YOU UNDER MY HOOD piston the night away OIL OF ME rambler man LOVE ME FENDER

ERNEST

UNCLASSIFIED

BUSINESS OPPORTUNITY

TAPE DISPENSER WHEELS.
Start your own retail gold mine. A great demand exists for these elusive disappearing wheels. Successful outlets are popping up in strip malls across the U. S. Franchises still available in most areas. For information call or write: Wheel of Good Fortune, P.O. Box 987, Roll Tide, Alabama. 1-800-GET-RICH.

FOR SALE

ELVIS POT HOLDERS.
That's right, the King lives. Complete line of Elvis Presley pot holders and oven mitts. Mitts used only when baking bread. Each comes with our letter of authenticity. For catalog send $50 to: Rack and Roll, Memphis, TN

FOR SALE

COWCUTTA STEAK KNIVES.
The finest stainless steel, handcrafted in India's largest industrial complex. Set of 4: $17.95. Family set of 28 only $24.95. Have credit card ready and call 1-800-S-L-I-C-E-I-T.

MISCELLANEOUS WANTED.

2 lb. Idaho potato that looks like Gerald Ford. Need to complete Presidential Potatohead collection. Must be in good condition. Call Nick Peeler (after 6:00 p.m. weekdays).

ERNEST

WANTED:

My other black lace-up wing tip shoes. Please mail soon. Cannot graduate without.

FOUND:

Blue kitty with retractable antennae. Answers to the name "Amal the night visitor."

LOST

My brother. Last seen wearing green corduroy body suit, talking to teddy bear with gruff voice. Drop him in any mailbox.

BUSINESS OPPORTUNITY

Deboner Entermanure seeks venture in pizza rental. Money no object, but a real problem.

TIMESHARE

Glorious climate, beautiful view, many weekends available. For more information call: 1-800-BIG-BOGG and ask for "Chainsaw Charlie"

CLASS TRIP TO WASHINGTON

Does your school class want to party hearty all the way to our nation's capital on a stuffy bus? Well, start packing because you're going, if you can pick up a golf tee. That's right, you and your class can recycle golf tees and be on your way in no time. Bending and stooping combined with super glue can make you Ms. or Mr. Tee before you know it.

THOUGHTS ON TOTS

IF SOMEONE BRINGS A REALLY UGLY BABY OVER TO YOUR HOUSE, YOU SHOULDN'T EVEN MENTION IT UNLESS YOU THINK IT MIGHT SCARE THE DOG.

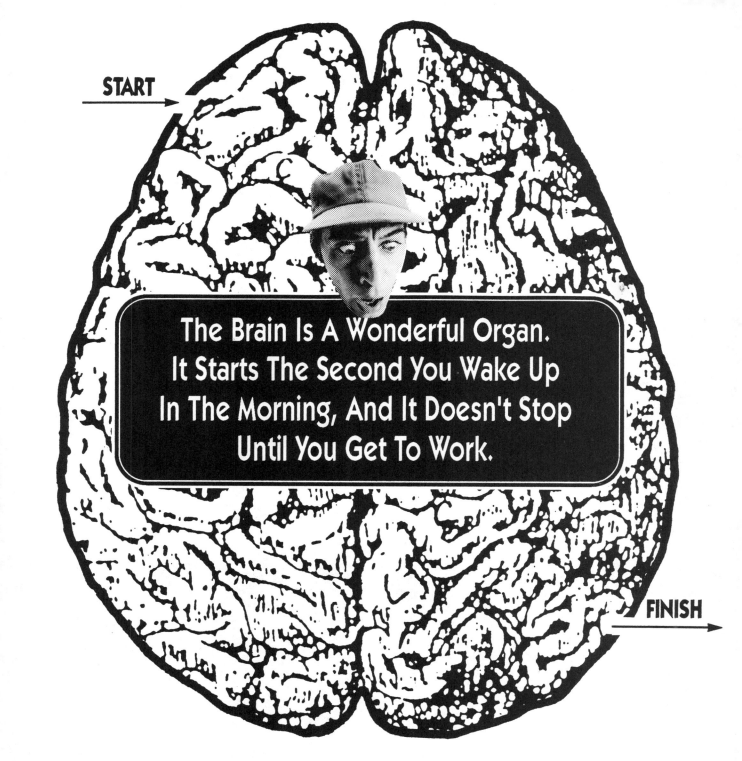

Good Manners

It's okay to make mashed potato sculptures at the dinner table, as long as you finish by the time the gravy comes around. I like to make a little castle with a moat for the gravy. Broccoli and parsley make dandy little shrubs.

The Word For The Day!

IGLOO

PRONOUNCED IG-GLUE: What you use when your **igs** are falling apart.

9 FUN WAYS TO HUMILIATE YOUR DOG.

1. Bathe them regularly.

2. Name the big ones "Fluffy and the little ones "Spike".

3. Pet them on the head real hard to watch their eyes get big.

4. Let them watch the first 25 minutes of Lassie, then change the channel to celebrity bowling.

5. Replace their food dish with a smaller one and misspell their names on it.

6. Always buy dry food in the 200 pound sack.

7. When playing "fetch," just pretend to throw a stick.

8. Give 'em a piece of bubble gum, a wad of taffy, or peanut butter crackers.

9. Call them just in time to let them see you eat that last bite of steak.

If
you take
a pig out of
the refrigerator for 3
days, you'll spoil him
rotten. Nevertheless, if you put
ham in a blender, some people won't
know what they are eating. And, if you take
the words "stork", "dork", and "New York", put them
in a little cellophane sack and seal it, you have a bag of
"Pork Rhymes".

Hey, Vern! If clothes make the man,
then naked people have no influence on society.

THINGS YOU SHOULD ASK YOURSELF...

...When you pick up your date:

Is my cap on straight?
Do I smell like onion rings?
Should I have left the dogs home?
Am I expected to tip her father?
At what point am I obligated to buy breakfast?

WEATHER

We're talkin' weatherhogs, Vern...better known as groundhogs or woodchucks. Usually the National Weather Service hogs all the credit, but the real meteorhogologists are underground. Their daily weather forecasting network is older than dirt.

The weatherhogs use a complex tunnel system that goes north, south, east and west...we're talkin' world-wide, Vern... with little holes venting the earth's surface. (You probably twisted your ankle in one playing yard darts in the backyard, Vern. By the way, Vern...they hate yard darts!)

Anyway, they stay busy running their reports back

ANXiETY

You can't live with it, you can't live without it.

- Standing in the checkout line at the grocery, knowing you're about to try and pass off expired coupons.
- Trying not to make eye contact with the charity solicitors standing outside of every store and airport in the country.
- Packing all your winter clothes in mothballs just as a cold front moves through the area.
- Getting that one bulbous zit a year... right on the tip of your nose...during the Christmas holidays.
- Pushing and pushing on a door that reads "Pull".
- Trying to guess which drive-in banking window is going to move the fastest.
- Following a car with its right blinker on for three miles only to have it finally turn...left.
- Filling out applications that require you to list every school you ever attended, credit references and doctor's addresses.
- Refusing to eat the first piece of bread in a loaf, then having to side-step it every time you want another slice.

Ernest P. Worrell's
Believe It or Else!

BOBBY T. WILLIAMSON

of French Lick, Indiana **ATE AN ENTIRE OUTBOARD MOTOR, INCLUDING THE STARTER CORD** DURING THE FIRST ACT OF THE FRENCH LICK FOUNDER'S DAY PAGEANT ON OCTOBER 3, 1978. BOBBY WAS IMMEDIATELY RUSHED TO HONEST AL'S GARAGE WHERE HE WAS AWARDED A FREE DINNER FOR FOUR AND SEVERAL SNACK PACKS OF SPARK PLUGS FOR HIS EFFORTS.

GULP!

SAM,

A FRESH WATER TROUT CAUGHT BY **ARNOLD ZERBISH** OF SIOUX CITY, IOWA, HAS STARTLED THE TOWNS-PEOPLE BY **ACTUALLY WHISTLING THE TUNE "OH SUSANNA!"** WHEN EVER HE WANTS HIS SUPPER!

...IT HAS BEEN DISCOVERED **MICHAELANGELO'S** CEILING OF THE SISTINE CHAPEL WAS ORIGINALLY COMPLETED THROUGH THE USE OF A **PAINT-BY-NUMBERS** SET THAT HE PURCHASED AT A FUND-RAISING AUCTION FOR A ROMAN SHOPPING MALL!

Is Slim Whitman Really the Bee Gee's Father?

Strange as it may seem, the warbling wonder fathered the three boys under intense medication in the late '70s. He later changed his name from Gibb to Whitman so as not to steal any success away from his kids. Slim, as music history has revealed, also co-wrote many of his son's hits which were originally titled: "Staying Alive Til The Check Clears The Bank" and "It's Saturday Night and I've Got A Fever." Since getting out of the recording business, Slim is marketing a new cheese spread called "Bee Gee Whiz." The boys have since acquired a lawyer from New York.

TO BE CONTINUED...

WEDDING RINGS
ARE USUALLY
CIRCULAR, AND
MEAN ETERNAL LOVE
AND COMMITMENT,
EVEN FOR YOUR
SECOND, THIRD, OR
FOURTH MARRIAGE.
NOT TO BE CONFUSED
WITH BATHTUB RINGS,
WHICH ARE A DIRTY
AND SORDID AFFAIR
IN THEMSELVES.

Love and Commitment

Farm Safety Tip Of The Month:

Do not try to teach a pig to sing. It will take up all your time and usually annoys the pig.

TAINT?

WHAT ACTUALLY IS

IT HAPPENS
EVERY YEAR. IT'S
AFTER WE OPEN ALL OUR
PRESENTS AND IT'S BEFORE WE
START ALL THOSE IMPOSSIBLE
RESOLUTIONS. IT'S WHEN WE'RE ALL WEARING
NEW SWEATERS, BUT WE HAVEN'T YET RECEIVED THE
CHARGE BILL FOR THEM. IT'S WHEN WE GO TO WORK BUT
NOBODY REALLY DOES ANYTHING. IT'S THOSE DAYS BETWEEN
CHRISTMAS AND NEW YEAR'S DAY. IT'S PURE HOLIDAY FUN BUT IT TAINT
CHRISTMAS AND IT TAINT NEW YEARS, IT'S JUST PLAIN TAINT.

KNOWHUTIMEAN?

The history of eggnog

Eggnog was first made in England in the late 1500's by William Shakespeare's second cousin Roy. Roy used to throw a dozen eggs, a handful of sugar and spice and a gallon of milk into a naugahyde bag (hence the Old English spelling "eggnaug") and set it out on his back porch overnight. The naugahyde would impart a wonderful flavor to the mixture, thus adding immensely to the holiday festivities.

Everything went great until the early 1900's when the Lazy Bob recliner was invented. Lazy Bob cornered the already small supply of naugahyde to cover their rockers. Thus, eggnaug faced possible extinction. That is, until Mrs. Beulah Horn of Flatwoods, Kentucky, suggested adding nutmeg to the mixture. The result was a smashing success, but much too late to change the name to Eggmeg.

Lazy Bob was so envious that they introduced a nutmeg recliner in 1928. They only sold three.

Weather Watch...
TROPICAL DEPRESSION

IT'S TIME FOR THAT CARIBBEAN VACATION. FIRST

STOP...MIAMI, WHERE YOU'LL PROBABLY CHANGE PLANES AND

YOUR LUGGAGE PROBABLY WON'T. SO WHILE YOU'RE

CHECKING IN TO THAT OVERPRICED HOTEL IN THE EXOTIC

ZONE, COLUMBIA DRUG ENFORCEMENT AGENTS WILL BE

CHECKING IN TO YOUR LUGGAGE AT THE BOGOTA

INTERNATIONAL AIRPORT. IT'S OK, DRUG AGENTS USUALLY

HAVE A GREAT SENSE OF HUMOR, AND SINCE YOU'LL BE ON

THE BEACH, WHO NEEDS A CHANGE OF CLOTHES, ANYWAY?

WRONG! THE BEACH ALWAYS WINS AND YOU WILL

EXPERIENCE THE WORST CASE OF SUNBURN KNOWN TO MAN.

THAT NICE RED LEATHER LOOK. TO COOL DOWN, YOU'LL DRINK

TOO MUCH LOCAL WATER AND YOU'LL SPEND THE REMAINDER

OF YOUR VACATION SEATED IN THE BATHROOM, STARING AT

YOUR ONLY PAIR OF UNDERWEAR AND WONDERING IF YOU'VE

MADE ANY NEW FRIENDS IN BOGOTA. ONLY AT THIS TIME

DOES ONE FULLY UNDERSTAND THE TRUE MEANING OF

"TROPICAL DEPRESSION."

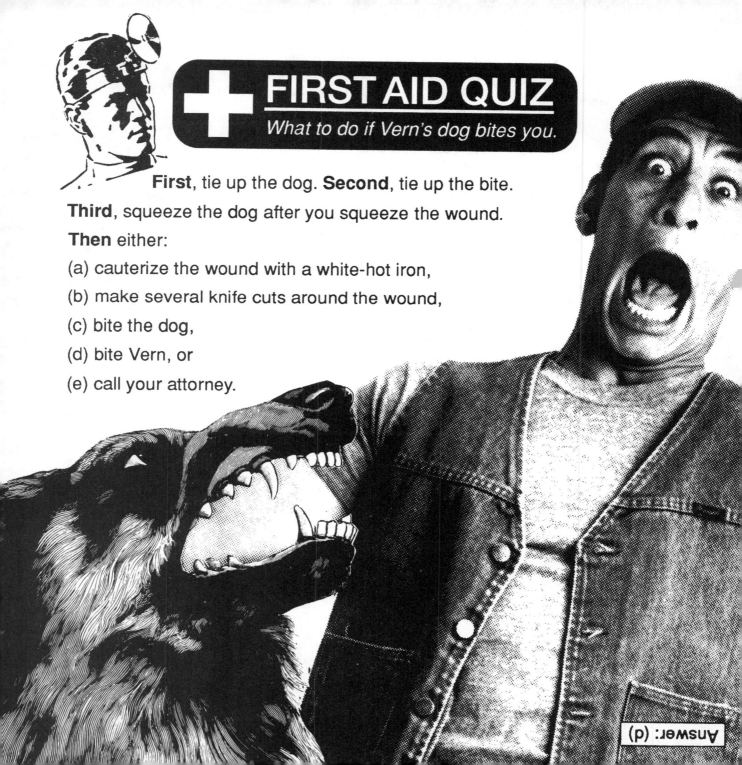

✚ FIRST AID QUIZ

What to do if Vern's dog bites you.

First, tie up the dog. **Second**, tie up the bite.

Third, squeeze the dog after you squeeze the wound.

Then either:

(a) cauterize the wound with a white-hot iron,

(b) make several knife cuts around the wound,

(c) bite the dog,

(d) bite Vern, or

(e) call your attorney.

Answer: (d)

Nine out of ten
Psychiatrists claim
that one out of four
people is crazy.
Check out three friends.
if they seem ok,
your it!

LOCUST SHELLS
FOR FUN AND PROFIT

This is a once in 13 years opportunity 'cause that's how long it is between locust attacks. If you've got them ugly bug shells all over your yard, start a collection. There's lots of ways to use 'em. Freeze some in ice cubes and invite the neighbors in for bug juice. Paint 'em red, put 'em on a string and save 'em for the Christmas tree. Paste a bunch on your fishing hat for good luck. And, best of all, if you can figure a way to keep 'em fresh for 13 years, you can put your bug shell collection all over your roof, so the next plague of locusts will think it's way too crowded at your place and go next door to Vern's house, KnoWhutImean?

HOW TO SEE THROUGH A WALL

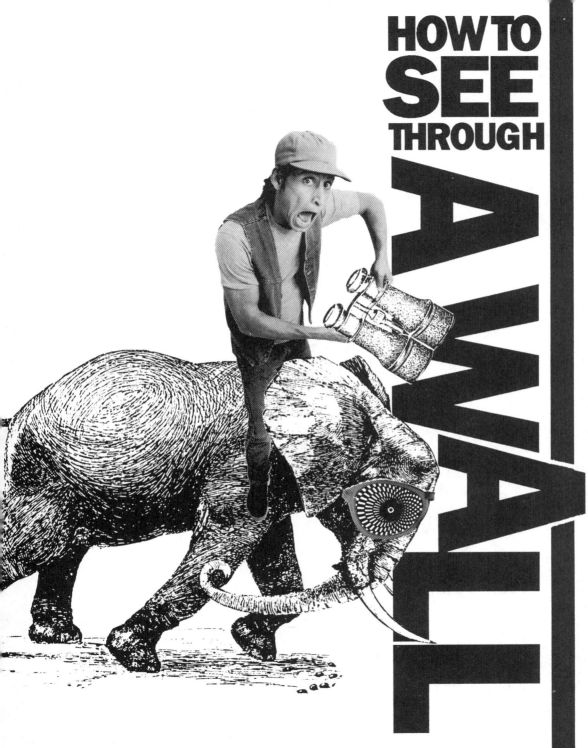

Your old buddy Ernest has tried several methods to accomplish this feat. Some success has been achieved by using X-Ray Glasses. You know, the ones that you find in your favorite comic book on the "Neat Junk To Order" page? The glasses are usually right there in between the U-Control 7-ft. Life-size Ghost and the Monkey-in-the-Teacup.

After years of trial and error with the X-Ray Glasses, try the proven Ernest P. Worrell method for seeing through walls: stand in front of a window.

HOME SAFETY TIPS

- Most accidents happen within 20 miles of home, so buy a cheap house and find something decent to rent about 21 miles away.
- Don't overload your kitchen's electrical outlets. If you have to, you can plug your blender in in the living room, and tell your guests it's a jacuzzi for your goldfish.
- Don't take chances with gas heat. Run a garden hose out your window and keep the inside end under your pillow at night. If gas escapes in your house, you'll have fresh air — and if it doesn't, you can always talk to your friends outside without getting out of bed.
- Never use the electric hedge trimmer to carve the turkey.
- It's okay to stir the gravy with the weed eater, but set the gravy on the floor first, and never stand on the table.
- Fly casting into the fish bowl can be good practice in the off season. Just be sure you're clear of all draperies and no one's standing behind you.
- A hot bath can put you to sleep. It's a good idea to put on your snorkel before you even get in the tub.

THINGS YOU SHOULD ASK YOURSELF...

...When you apply for a job:

Is this really necessary?
Am I really broke?
Why is there an opening if this is such a good job?
Do I have to lift anything heavier than a paycheck?
How long before I'm eligible for a vacation?
How long before I'm eligible for unemployment?
Is this really necessary?

THINGS YOUR MOTHER TOLD YOU
MYTHS...

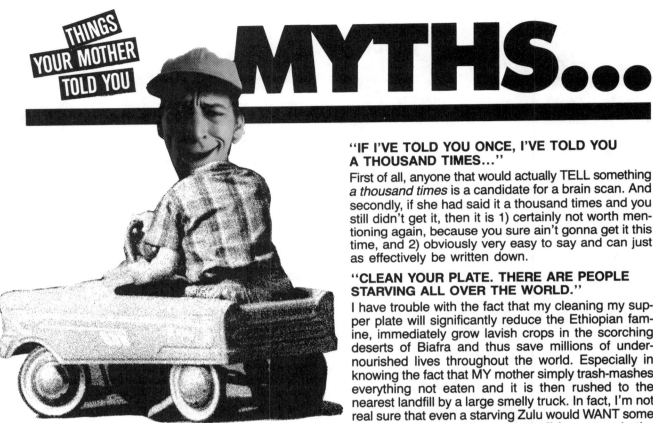

"ALWAYS WEAR CLEAN UNDERWEAR. YOU MIGHT BE IN A WRECK."

This is, of course, ridiculous. The connection between clean underwear and the possibility of a serious traffic accident occurring is, for one thing, completely unfounded and simply an unwarranted consideration. Should you be in a wreck, the chances of the ambulance attendant saying, "Hey, Chuck, we ain't helpin' this schmuck. Look everybody, check out this clown's underwear," are, at best, very slim. The fashion factor involved in a car wreck barely makes the meter. Though it has been scientifically proven that the presence of clean underwear can relate directly to the approval of a large trailer home loan.

"IF I'VE TOLD YOU ONCE, I'VE TOLD YOU A THOUSAND TIMES..."

First of all, anyone that would actually TELL something *a thousand times* is a candidate for a brain scan. And secondly, if she had said it a thousand times and you still didn't get it, then it is 1) certainly not worth mentioning again, because you sure ain't gonna get it this time, and 2) obviously very easy to say and can just as effectively be written down.

"CLEAN YOUR PLATE. THERE ARE PEOPLE STARVING ALL OVER THE WORLD."

I have trouble with the fact that my cleaning my supper plate will significantly reduce the Ethiopian famine, immediately grow lavish crops in the scorching deserts of Biafra and thus save millions of undernourished lives throughout the world. Especially in knowing the fact that MY mother simply trash-mashes everything not eaten and it is then rushed to the nearest landfill by a large smelly truck. In fact, I'm not real sure that even a starving Zulu would WANT some of what my mother has passed off for supper in the past. I've found the best retort to this silly line of reasoning to be either "Fine, I'll pay postage," or the conversation-stopping "Name two of them."

"THIS IS GOING TO HURT ME A LOT MORE THAN IT IS YOU."

This, of course, usually comes on the front end of inflicting physical pain on you either manually or with the aid of outside means. The fallacy is obvious. The only time this came true for me was when the double-pump 30.06 shotgun Mother was aiming at me for leaving my socks in the hallway backfired through the chamber, annihilating a third of her face and most of her neck. But as a rule this one just doesn't hold.

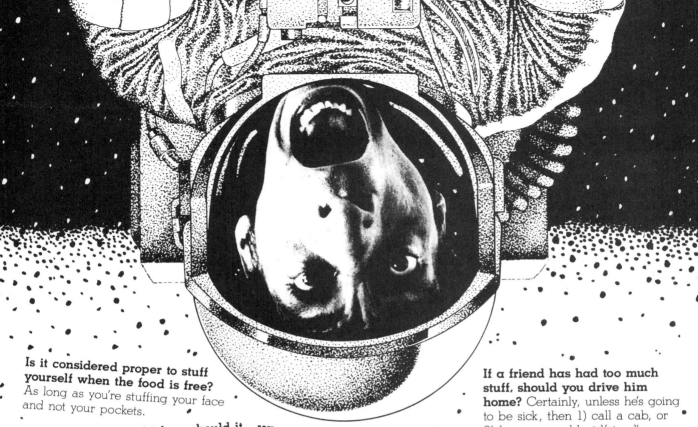

Is it considered proper to stuff yourself when the food is free? As long as you're stuffing your face and not your pockets.

After stuffing a chicken, should it be placed on a roasting pan or on the mantle? Roasting pan if stuffed with cornbread; on the mantle if stuffed with baby pictures.

What do you do when surrounded by stuffed shirts? Strike up a conversation on the new blender parts surveyed in the latest edition of *Consumer Reports* magazine.

How do you tell good stuff from bad stuff? Poke it with a stick, but never, ever, put your lips on it.

When is the correct time to strut your stuff? Just after successfully executing a 7-10 split.

How do you recognize Mr. Big Stuff? Two-tone Lincoln Continental Mark IV, bad cigar, smelly toupe, waiting for large fries at McDonald's Drive-Thru.

If you stuff a basketball, will it explode? No, but you do get two points and a chance to run the length of the court.

If a friend has had too much stuff, should you drive him home? Certainly, unless he's going to be sick, then 1) call a cab, or 2) borrow an old girlfriend's car.

How do you avoid the rough stuff? Always carry a belt sander and a three-prong adapter.

Is your stuff tough enough? No.

What if someone wants to knock the stuffing out of you? See Stuffed Shirts.

What if they make fun of your stuff? Tell 'em where they can stuff it!

THE RIGHT STUFF

AIRPORT ETIQUETTE

DON'T
take your pocket
KNIFE

collection with you...
'cause you'll never get
past the X-ray machine...
and the security
GUARDS
will take you to a little
room without windows...
and make you empty
your various pockets full
of assorted knives...
while your family
LEAVES
on a flight to Florida for
4 days and 3 nights...
which is how long it'll
take you to
EXPLAIN
why it was so important
to take all those pocket
knives to Sea World
anyway.

Do put an alarm clock in
your suitcase and set it
so it'll be ringing when
you get to the baggage
claim. Most of the
crowd will clear out
immediately and you'll
find your stuff real easy.

BUTLER'S "WALTONIAN"

THINGS YOU SHOULD KNOW ABOUT

THE LAUNDROMAT ➤ ➤ ➤

THINGS YOU SHOULD KNOW ABOUT THE LAUNDROMAT

It happens to all of us at one time or another, Vern. No matter how careful we are or how dainty we are in our personal habits, every six months or so even the neatest of us has to break down and go wash our clothes. Unless you live near a handy waterfall or it happens to be the monsoon season, that usually means you're gonna have to make a trip to the local laundromat. If you haven't ever been there before, you'll want to tattoo these valuable little laundromat tips on your brain for future reference.

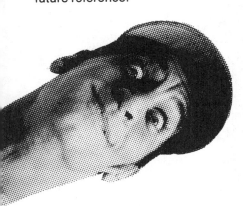

MACHINES

You'll find all kinds of machines at the laundromat, Vern, but you got to be careful 'cause not all of them are gonna help clean your clothes:

• DETERGENT SLOT MACHINE

This is a gambling machine some of the better laundromats install to help you pass the time. All you do is put in a quarter and pull down on the slot machine handle and, if you're lucky, you'll win a little bitty box of detergent that looks just like the big boxes they sell in the grocery stores. It's loads of fun, Vern, and these little boxes can come in real handy because if you toss one of them into a washing machine with your clothes, it will sometimes foam up just like real detergent, and I even think it helps get your clothes cleaner. Of course, you usually have to brush the cardboard off your clothes when you're done.

• CHANGE MACHINE

This is another machine to help you pass the time. What you do is put in a dollar bill and (believe it or not) the machine sorta *sucks* the dollar bill inside itself for a second, then it shoves it back out at you and a little light comes on saying "Out Of Order." You can while away a lot of time playing with one of these machines, Vern, but I gotta warn you that every so often your dollar bill will go into the machine and you'll hear a great big "Clunk" and then a sound will come that sounds like a bunch of metal washers dropping into a coffee can and your dollar won't come back again. That's your signal to change machines, which is where this particular machine gets its name, I guess.

• IRONING MACHINES

This machine looks like a couple of little ironing boards hinged together to make a kind of sandwich. What you do is put a coin into it and the machine will make a kind of hissing noise and the top half of the machine will clomp down on the bottom half for a couple of seconds. To tell you the truth, Vern, I ain't really sure what this machine is supposed to do, although I have found it comes in real handy for re-heating fast food burgers (only you got to remember to take them out of the styrofoam box first.)

HOW TO LOAD A WASHING MACHINE

All laundromat washing machines have signs saying "DO NOT OVERLOAD," but how is a layman to know how much is too much? The answer's simple, Vern.

Since your clothes are all gonna wind up in the dryer when you're finished, a dryer-full means one full load. So before you stuff your clothes in the washer, stick them into a dryer and see how many you can cram in. The amount you wind up with is how much you should put in the washer…one load.

(Although you really gotta figure that a washer-full is a little less than one full load when you take into account that your clothes will probably be 25% lighter when they're clean.)

THINGS YOU SHOULD KNOW ABOUT THE LAUNDROMAT

THE KIND OF PEOPLE YOU MEET IN THE LAUNDROMAT

- Clean, neat people who come in once a week.
- Not·so·clean, neat people who come in once a month.
- Not·so·clean, not·so·neat people who come in only before having company over.
- Not·so·clean, real un-neat people who come in only by court order.

WHAT TO DO WHILE YOUR CLOTHES ARE WASHING

Chit-chat with the other patrons about the joys of laundry. Here're some conversation starters:

"I noticed that you wash your underwear with your washcloths. Don't that sometimes give you the shivers?"

"How much luck have you been having trying to mix your delicates and fine washables with canvas lawn chair backs?"

"How many socks you figure you've lost in here over the years?"

"Since the machine stops every time you lift the lid up, how do we know we're gettin' our money's worth?"

WHAT TO DO IF YOU TAKE SOMEBODY ELSE'S CLOTHES HOME

1. See if they fit. Sometimes an accident like this is just Fate's way of telling you that you need a change in your lifestyle.
2. Hold a yard sale.
3. Go back to the laundromat and stuff the other person's clothes in an empty dryer and go find your own.

WHAT TO DO IF SOMEBODY TAKES YOUR CLOTHES HOME BY ACCIDENT

This has never happened to me, Vern. I guess I'm just protected by a higher and wiser power.

PICKING A LAUNDROMAT

First thing to look for when you pick a laundromat is to look and see if there's a video arcade nearby. If you can't find a laundromat with a video arcade, then look for one near a grocery store because one thing you're gonna need a lot of at the laundromat is quarters and dimes. (Or is that *two* things?)

'Course, a video arcade is the easiest and best place to get quarters, but a grocery store will do if you're doing your laundry in a socially deprived neighborhood without videodromes.

Sometimes, the clerk at the grocery store won't want to give you four dollars worth of quarters, so you have to use your IN-JOO-NEW-ITEE. (That means burnin' brain cells, Vern.)

Go up to the clerk and try one of these reasons for needin' so many quarters.

- My right leg is shorter than the other and I need quarters for ballast.
- There's a TV crew secretly watching us to see who is the most accommodating checkout clerk in town.
- My religion don't allow me to handle paper money.
- I have to keep a strict accounting of my money on hand, but all the keys on my pocket calculator except ¼ have burned out.
- I want to buy all the prizes that come in those gumball-kinda machines by the door and send the prizes off to children in foreign lands.
- I have to make a station-to-station call to Iceland from a phone booth to prevent dysentery from spreadin'.

PICTURE PUZZLE

Game A. ERNEST SUFFERS FROM DEJA VU
OBJECT: Help Ernest find his way to Vern's.
RULES: Ernest must go around each obstacle once and only once - nor may
he cross his own path. To determine winner, use a string or ruler and
follow path as drawn. You cannot go out of the border. Color drawings as
you go. In case of tie, replay game using eggtimer set at 2 minutes.
GAME B. FIND THE MISSING BUFFALO

WHERE THE BOYS ARE:

Homer,	Alaska
Clifton,	Arizona
Norman,	Arkansas
Arnold,	California
Craig,	Colorado
Warren,	Connecticut
Milton,	Delaware
Bruce,	Florida
Buford,	Georgia
Papa,	Hawaii
Boise,	Idaho
Raymond,	Illinois
Arthur,	Indiana
Spencer,	Iowa
Chester,	Kansas
Clay,	Kentucky
Archibald,	Louisiana
Perry,	Maine
Frederick,	Maryland
Newton,	Massachusetts
Glennie,	Michigan
Russell,	Minnesota
Allen,	Mississippi
Herman,	Missouri
Troy,	Montana
Stuart,	Nebraska
Nelson,	Nevada
Webster,	New Hampshire
Franklin,	New Jersey
Anthony,	New Mexico
Victor,	New York
Harvey,	North Dakota
Conway,	North Carolina
Napolean,	Ohio
Duncan,	Oklahoma
Brothers,	Oregon
Tyrone,	Pennsylvania
Vernon,	Rhode Island
Elliott,	South Carolina

MAKE CHEESE

All you need is milk, rennet (if you can't rennet, buy it)...and bacteria! It's simple, just keep the mixture in a cool dark place and when the germs die, the cheese is done. So if we make enough cheese – we can rid the world of disease. Then we can devote more time and energy perfecting 900 numbers and midget wrestling.

EXTENDED FORECAST

FALL:

Temps fall fast, Curly - get your fishin' in early!

WINTER:

Cool, Cold, 'n Colder (but not Coldest) - get your taters 'n wheat in the ground.

SPRING:

Way too much rain - wait till Good Friday to plant a Good Garden.

SUMMER:

It's gonna be hot all over! Water your 'maters, dust off your flip-flops and your little brother, then head to the beach!

Eatie Gourmet Picks The Platters

"Whistle A Happy Tuna"

"Olive Paris In The Springtime"

"Sole Man"

"Two Loaves have I"

"Olive Me"

"Olive You Truly"

"Peelings"

"Up, Up And A-Whey"

"Home On The Range"

"Liver, Come Back To Me"

"I Flounder A New Baby"

THE EIGHT WONDERS OF THE WORLD.

You know, Vern, I'm always wonderin'. Wonderin' this and wonderin' that. KnoWhutImean?

Well, the other day I sat down and figured what the eight wonders I wondered the most were.

Do you ever find yourself wonderin', Vern?

I wonder why?

1. I wonder if thin cows give skim milk?

2. I wonder how a thermos bottle knows whether to keep it hot or cold?

3. I wonder if the Pyramids of Egypt would still be standing if they had been built with the pointy end down? Or if that's the angle to take at all?

4. I wonder if the Great Wall of China ever had a Great Roof or Great Coffee Tables? Or I wonder if they were just Good?

5. I wonder if the Hanging Gardens of Babylon used giant macrame holders? Or if Nebuchadnezzar just had one heck of green thumb? Were there any weedeaters? How did tomato plants do back then?

6. I wonder if the Empire State Building is jealous of the World Trade Center?

7. I wonder which one would get the most tourists and sell the most postcards if Niagara Falls was in the Grand Canyon? Could you get your picture taken in front of both at the same time?

8. I wonder if the Presidents on the face of Mount Rushmore ever get height sickness? Did they have to sign model releases? How did they get them all together for the picture?

THINGS MY MOTHER NEVER TOLD ME ABOUT...

ABOUT DOGS: When dogs get "fixed", the chances of them ever seeing their grandchild are greatly reduced. This, to me, seems a misnomer. Shouldn't it be "broken"?

ABOUT EAR WAX: Interchangeable with toe jam. In fact, Q-tips work well at both ends of your body.

ABOUT SEX: She never told me anything, and my cousin didn't know anything. I've heard it's alive and well and living somewhere east of Omaha.

FLY FISHING

*"Fly fishing isn't a sport
Fly fishing is an art..."*
The Urban Sportsman Magazine

- Always use only the tiniest, itty-bitty lures. Flies' mouths are not very big and large lures only confuse them.

- Fish in areas that you know to be breeding and spawning grounds for species of flies: municipal landfills, family picnics, city zoos, etc. In fact, if you have a dog and a little imagination, you can have your own secret spot.

- Camouflage clothing is always a good bet, especially when decked for fishing in a double-breasted watermelon suit.

- Take precautions when removing the hook from the fly. After all, the little guy has been through a lot and he might just completely come apart.

- Gutting and skinning the kill can be hassle-free with the aid of an 8 lb. ballpeen hammer. Mounting on the front of your car for transport, though, is not recommended. Always remember, keep what you can eat and release the rest.

148751

THE TRUTH ABOUT JACK FROST

Now, the shortest alcoholic at the Tulsa, Oklahoma Vagrants' Mission, the legendary Jack Frost, was, in fact, once a man of high prestige and honor. Jack, you see, was the Official Barber of the North Pole. Jack applied for this prestigious position shortly after his heart-wrenching and devastating break-up with long time friend and songwriting partner, Jill (see "Nursery Rhymes We Never Knew"). Not taking into consideration his disdain for winter sports, the very poor television reception and short-lived excitement every December, trimming the facial hair of Santa and his non-union elves was simply not enough to keep Jack content.

It was only a matter of time before Jack started hitting the spiked egg nog. And hitting it hard. Top management could overlook this unelf-like behavior until that tragic day...the day Jack, in a drunken stupor, inadvertantly clipped the end of Santa's nose while trimming his mustache. After six long weeks in a grueling elf trial, Jack "The Nipper" was found guilty of negligence in duty and was sentenced to five years of making frosted mugs in an Irish pub. Luckily for Jack, the pub was owned and managed by his cousin, Jack O'Lantern.

When Jack had finally paid his debt to the Santa Society, he returned to his first true love: breeding rabbits in the desert Southwest. But the ruins of alcohol had taken their toll and Jack's chemical dependence on the wicked juice won out over all sense of honor and duty. The rabbits never had a chance.

Today, Jack is all but forgotten at the North Pole, remembered only in his mention in the now-famous wintertime song put together by the elves to future generations of his mishap with Santa..."Jack Frost nipping at your nose..." Those crazy elves...

PLANE TRUTH

EVERYONE ON THE PLANE PAID LESS THAN YOU DID.

DON'T RIDE IN AIRPLANES WITH PILOTS NAMED SNOOKIE OR BINX.

IF YOU'RE SERVED A MEAL ON THE PLANE, SAVE YOURSELF A LOT OF TIME AND ENERGY AND PUT THE FOOD DIRECTLY IN THE AIR SICKNESS BAG IN FRONT OF YOU.

My Favorite Vacation Spots

Gerald Martin's MEAT 'N' THREE

My favorite wintertime fun spot is right outside Minnagua, Wisconsin. It's known for trapping, but the last few years the big attraction has been a humongous pack of 3-legged dogs. There's lots of dogs in the area, so when you combine that with lots of traps, you get lots of 3-legged dogs. Gerald's been taking them in now for about 15 years. Even in heavy snow, the road to Gerald's is marked real good. You can't miss it. It's kind of like following the yellow brick road. KnoWhutImean?

Earl Gateland's SQUIRT-A-RAMA

Just 30 miles southeast of Riverton, Wyoming, stands a monument to American ingenuity. A full-size dairy barn made entirely of Squirt soft drink bottles. They don't make Squirt Soda any more, so Earl's architectural wonder never really had a chance to catch on. You might wanna bring camping gear since there aren't any motels closer than Riverton, but if there aren't more than 5 or 6 of you, Earl and Emily would be glad to put you up in their house.

Tornado Observation and Mobile Home Park

For a really exciting vacation, I head about 20 miles north of Hutchinson, Kansas, where the National Weather Service has their tornado observatory. They use a small mobile home park for bait, and if you get there during the peak tornado season (March-August), chances are real good you'll see one. Lodging is no problem. In fact, the weather service usually has trouble filling the trailers during peak season.

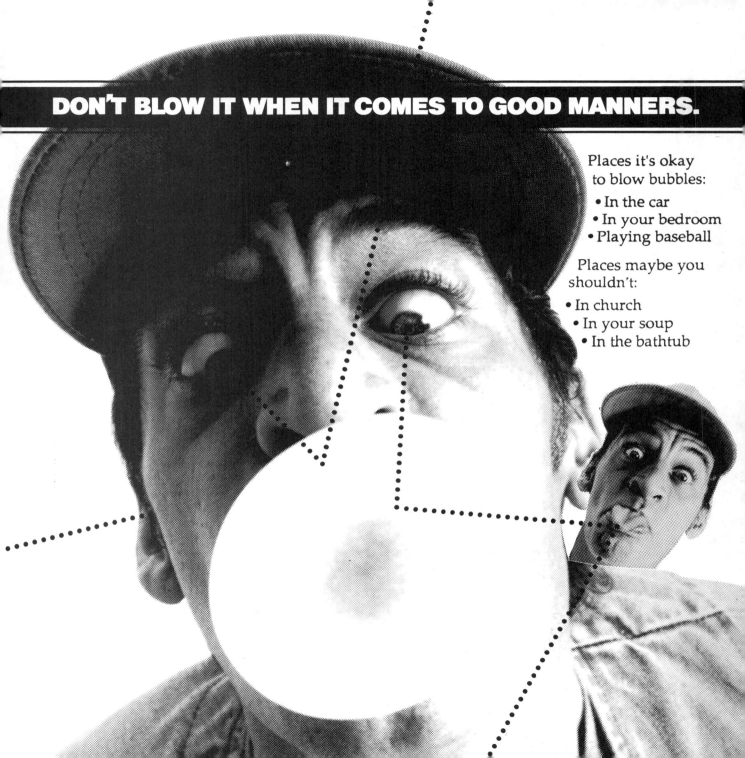

DON'T BLOW IT WHEN IT COMES TO GOOD MANNERS.

Places it's okay
to blow bubbles:
- In the car
- In your bedroom
- Playing baseball

Places maybe you
shouldn't:
- In church
- In your soup
- In the bathtub

What You WANTED

What You ACTUALLY GOT

FOR CHRISTMAS

FOR CHRISTMAS

What You Wanted	What You Actually Got
A PONY	A BATHROBE
ALLEN WRENCHES	SAVINGS BOND
COLOR TV	ENCYCLOPEDIA
LEATHER JACKET	VINYL JACKET
INVISIBLE WOMAN	INVISIBLE MAN
SEASON BASEBALL TICKETS	MILITARY SCHOOL
BOX OF CHOCOLATES	LICORICE
MINK COAT	HAND-KNIT SWEATER 3 SIZES TOO BIG
A CAR	GALOSHES
BB GUN	ANOTHER SAVINGS BOND
BARBIE'S DREAM HOUSE	A LITTLE BROTHER
YOUR OWN ROOM	BUNK BEDS
CLEAR SKIN	SHOESHINE KIT
ETCH-A-SKETCH	3-RING BINDER
G. I. JOE	FRUITCAKE
MAGNUM P. I. CALENDAR	TOOTHBRUSH
DOG	TURTLE
COWBOY BOOTS	SOCKS
VIEW MASTER	TRAVEL SEWING KIT
HAWAIIAN SHIRT	YELLOW RAIN COAT
TRIP TO DISNEYLAND	TRIP TO THE DENTIST
VCR	ONE MORE SAVINGS BOND

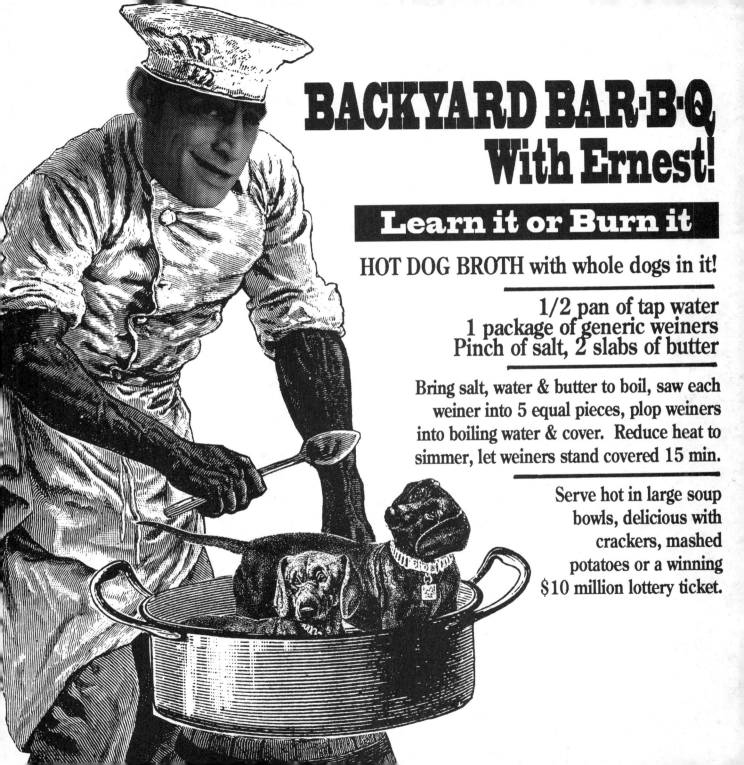

BACKYARD BAR-B-Q With Ernest!

Learn it or Burn it

HOT DOG BROTH with whole dogs in it!

1/2 pan of tap water
1 package of generic weiners
Pinch of salt, 2 slabs of butter

Bring salt, water & butter to boil, saw each weiner into 5 equal pieces, plop weiners into boiling water & cover. Reduce heat to simmer, let weiners stand covered 15 min.

Serve hot in large soup bowls, delicious with crackers, mashed potatoes or a winning $10 million lottery ticket.

CAMPER'S POINTERS

► Bug sprays and insect repellents don't always work when there's a zillion mosquitoes for each camper. Bring extra sleeping bags and a mannequin head for each bag. Smear some ground beef on the mannequin's face and sprinkle some inside the bag (about 1 lb. per bag). By the time the mosquitoes figure out they've been tricked, you should be able to catch a few winks before you have to start swatting again. Note: If you're on a tight budget, Spam will work as your decoy meat with some of your dumber varieties of mosquitoes.

► Learn the difference between poison ivy and toilet paper.

► Try to leave the woods a safer place than you found it. Bring along a few small, inexpensive fire extinguishers, and just nail one to a tree every now and then when the mood hits you.

► If a snake bites you and you're far from civilization, ask a fellow to suck the poison out. Don't ask someone who owes you a lot of money. Ask someone who you owe.

► Borrow money from your fellow campers, and pay them back promptly at the end of the trip.

► Sitting around the campfire can get a little boring after a couple of days. Try to bring along at least one person who hasn't heard all your stories. A big guy who likes to carry things.

► If you think there might be bears in the area, tune your radio to a heavy metal station and turn it all the way up. Bears hate heavy metal music. Most of them think they quit making good music after the early 60's. Note: This will also help to drown out those annoying bird sounds you hear early in the morning.

IN ONE DAY,
SAMSON KILLED
A THOUSAND PHILISTINES
WITH THE JAWBONE
OF AN ASS.

EVERY DAY,
A THOUSAND DEALS
ARE KILLED WITH
THE SAME WEAPON.

AMERICANS DRIVE 65 M.P.H. ON THE FREEWAYS AND EVERYTHING GOES BY PRETTY QUICK. SO, WE MUST TAKE SOME TIME TO BRUSH UP ON THE NUMBERING SYSTEM OF THE INTERSTATE HIGHWAYS.

AN EVEN-NUMBERED INTERSTATE RUNS EAST AND WEST WITH LOW-NUMBERED ONES IN THE SOUTH AND HIGH-NUMBERED ONES IN THE NORTH. AN ODD-NUMBERED INTERSTATE RUNS NORTH AND SOUTH WITH THE LOW NUMBERS IN THE WEST AND HIGH NUMBERS IN THE EAST. NOW, AN INTERSTATE WITH 3 DIGITS MEANS YOU ARE ON A LOOP OR A BELTWAY AND YOU'RE PROBABLY GOING IN CIRCLES.

IT ALL KIND OF MAKES SENSE UNTIL YOU GET TO HAWAII WHERE THEIR "INTERSTATE" HIGHWAYS DON'T CONNECT WITH ANY ON THE MAINLAND.

SEEMS THERE'S TOO MUCH TALK ABOUT NUMBERS HERE. THIS MIGHT TURN INTO A MATH THING IF WE'RE NOT CAREFUL... BETTER GO ON TO THE NEXT PAGE, JUST TO PLAY IT SAFE.

TV Holiday Specials We'd Like To See!

NONE. ZIP. BLANK. ZERO. GET OUT OF HERE. HOW 'BOUT SOME EXTRA PRO FOOTBALL INSTEAD.

Always Follow The Leader To Good Table Manners

When your host offers you corn-on-the-cob, don't roll it on the butter stick unless they do it first. The same goes for black olives: Don't put one on each finger tip and suck it unless they do it first.

Why is Mona Lisa Smiling?

POP QUIZ

A. She's sitting on a blue Whoopie Cushion.

B. Her divorce came through and she gets to keep the Volvo.

C. She's under gas from a root canal operation.

D. There's a little "hanger" in Da Vinci's nose.

E. She passed her urine test.

F. She's not smiling, she didn't get the Volvo.

QUESTIONS

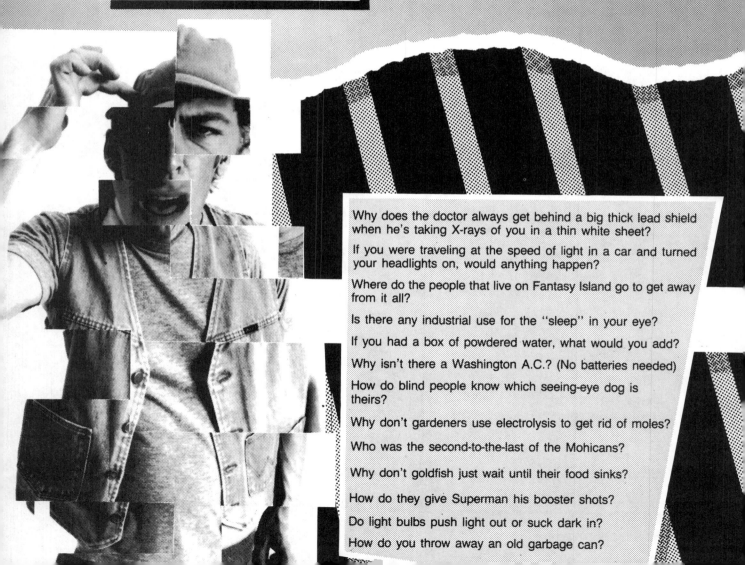

Why does the doctor always get behind a big thick lead shield when he's taking X-rays of you in a thin white sheet?

If you were traveling at the speed of light in a car and turned your headlights on, would anything happen?

Where do the people that live on Fantasy Island go to get away from it all?

Is there any industrial use for the "sleep" in your eye?

If you had a box of powdered water, what would you add?

Why isn't there a Washington A.C.? (No batteries needed)

How do blind people know which seeing-eye dog is theirs?

Why don't gardeners use electrolysis to get rid of moles?

Who was the second-to-the-last of the Mohicans?

Why don't goldfish just wait until their food sinks?

How do they give Superman his booster shots?

Do light bulbs push light out or suck dark in?

How do you throw away an old garbage can?

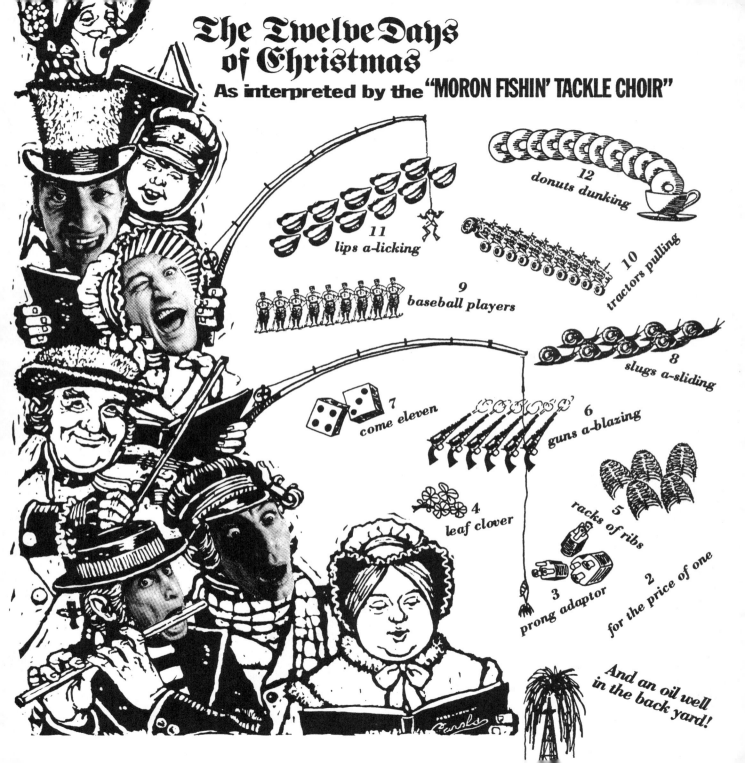

??? **Picture Puzzle** ???

Which bunny is different?

A.

B.

C.

<u>Answer:</u> Bunny D (not pictured) is left-handed
and lives in Detroit.

The TOP TEN Favorite Christmas Carols.

1. Jingle Bell Rock
2. We Three Kings Beat Two of a Kind
3. Santa Claus Conquers the Martians
4. Oh Little Town of Graceland
5. We Wish You a Mahvelous Christmas Dahling
6. Tan Your Bottom
7. Revenge of the Nerd Elvis
8. Any song on the "Christmas with Rosemary Clooney" Album
9. The 365 Days of Christmas
10. Inna-Godda-Da-Vida (The long version)

The Ernest P. Worrell Complete List of Games Even Vern Can Master.

THE THRILL OF VICTORY

Bobbing for Water.
Sighted Man's Bluff.
Chicken Croquette.
Pin the Tail on the Wall.
Ring Around the Toilet.
Hop Scotch with a Splash.
Standing in Place.
Touch Your Knee.
Guess Your Age.
Connect the Dot.
52-Card Stud.
Sleep Frog.
Catch a Cold.

• **Self-service gas stations with 25¢ air machines.** • **Refusing to answer the phone while in the shower, but finally you run, dripping wet, answer the phone and a small child goes "Ernie? Ernie Dinklefwat?"** • **Getting Christmas cards from people you don't know.** • **Receiving your Publisher's Clearing House Sweepstakes Mailer.** • **Having a dentist named Dr. Blood.** • **Discovering you can't open a child-proof bottle.** • **Running out of Halloween candy just as the Rosewood Demons come knocking at your door.** • **Asking people what they think of your haircut and they say "it's different."** • **Finding the perfect apartment, and it's got shag carpeting... in avocado.** • **Realizing that the last parking space at the mall is for the handicapped.** • **Being asked by your visiting aunt to go upstairs and get her teeth.**

Summer Survival Techniques

STAY COOL WITH CHILI
SALSA — WHEN YOUR
INSIDES STEAM UP,
THE VAPORS COOL OFF
YOUR OUTSIDES.

IT'S BEST TO EAT
CUCUMBERS IN MONTHS
SPELT WITH A "U".

CHOOSE A VACATION SPOT
WHERE SHIRTS AND SHOES
ARE NOT REQUIRED.

NEVER WEAR WING TIPS
INSTEAD OF WATER WINGS.

IF THE YOUNG'NS GET
RESTLESS, TELL 'EM TO
UNFOLD THE LAWN CHAIRS.

For FUN and PROFIT learn to MOUNT BIRDS

Fowlodermistry, a proven path to fun and profit, could change your life today. With little effort, you too can become an entremanure. With the "back to nature" attitudes of people in the know, fowl items are in hot demand. Picture yourself creating such works as: the Flaming Albatross Choker, the Coveted Hummingbird Broach – just to name a few. And with Interior Designers screaming for the Art Ducko look, success is at your fingertips. Because, Vern, the price of down is going up.

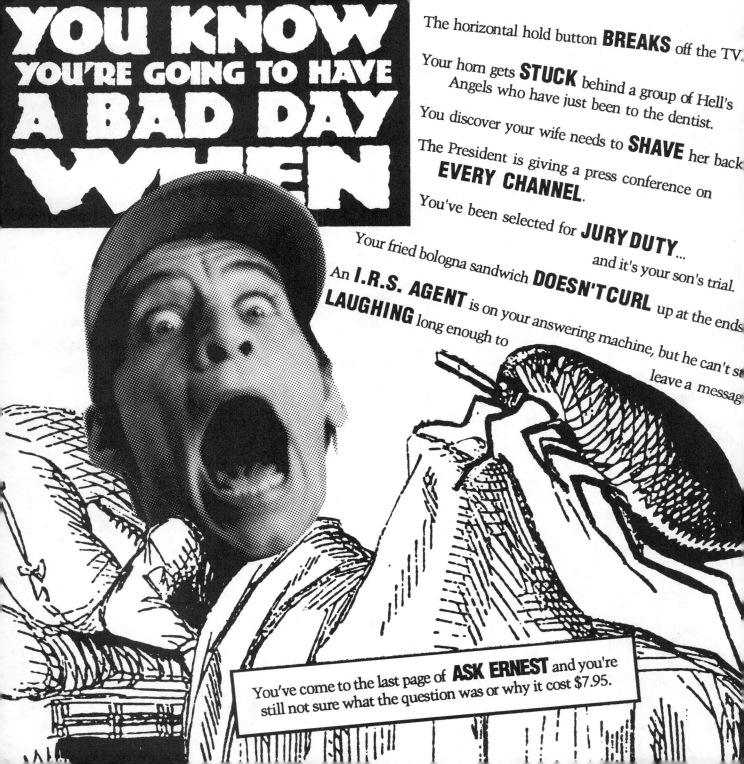

YOU KNOW YOU'RE GOING TO HAVE A BAD DAY WHEN

The horizontal hold button **BREAKS** off the TV.

Your horn gets **STUCK** behind a group of Hell's Angels who have just been to the dentist.

You discover your wife needs to **SHAVE** her back

The President is giving a press conference on **EVERY CHANNEL**.

You've been selected for **JURY DUTY**... and it's your son's trial.

Your fried bologna sandwich **DOESN'T CURL** up at the ends

An **I.R.S. AGENT** is on your answering machine, but he can't st **LAUGHING** long enough to leave a messag

You've come to the last page of **ASK ERNEST** and you're still not sure what the question was or why it cost $7.95.